The Arabian Gulf Economic & Investment Ecosystem

Unfold the Arabian Gulf Countries Economic & Investment Landscape

Bahaa G Arnouk

ISBN: 978-1-0685581-2-2

Book Cover by Bahaa Arnouk

1st edition 2024

Table of contents

Introduction

The Gulf region, a tapestry woven from ancient traditions and modern aspirations, stands as a testament to economic dynamism. Blessed with abundant hydrocarbon resources, these nations are acutely aware of the imperative to transcend the limitations of a single resource-dependent model. This book embarks on a journey through the economic and investment landscapes of six key players in this region: Saudi Arabia, Qatar, Oman, the United Arab Emirates, Kuwait, and Iraq. This book will uncover the unique tapestry of each nation, revealing the intricate interplay of opportunities and challenges that define their investment climates.

From the ambitious giga-projects reshaping Saudi Arabia's horizon to the echoes of the World Cup still resonating through Qatar's burgeoning tourism sector, each country narrates a compelling story of transformation. We'll delve into Oman's steady march towards a diversified future, powered by renewable energy and a burgeoning logistics network, and explore the UAE's unwavering ascent as a global hub for innovation and investment. Kuwait's unique challenge of balancing abundant wealth with the urgency for structural reform will be examined, as will Iraq's inspiring journey of reconstruction and its push towards a private sector-driven economy.

This book does not merely present a snapshot of the present; it provides a roadmap for navigating the future. Each chapter equips readers with the knowledge and insights needed to assess risks, seize opportunities, and make informed investment decisions in a region pulsating with potential.

Prepare to immerse yourself in the intricate economic fabric of the Gulf, where ancient wisdom converges with modern ambition, and where discerning investors can find fertile ground for growth and prosperity.

CHAPTER 1

Saudi Arabia's Metamorphosis: From Oil Giant to Global Investment Hub

Step into a land where the echoes of ancient caravans meet the pulse of cutting-edge technology. Saudi Arabia, a nation undergoing a vibrant metamorphosis, is writing a new chapter in its story, fuelled by the ambitious Vision 2030. This chapter captures this captivating evolution – a delicate dance between ambition and opportunity. From futuristic cities rising from the desert floor to a burgeoning tech scene rivalling established hubs, Saudi Arabia beckons investors seeking growth and a stake in a transformative journey. But like any intricate tapestry, the threads of complexity are woven into this narrative. Let's navigate Kingdom's economic landscape together, uncovering not just the dazzling potential but also the nuances that demand a discerning eye.

Beyond the Oil Fields: Charting Saudi Arabia's Diversification Success

While the black gold has long fuelled its economic engine, Saudi Arabia is proactively crafting a new destiny, diversifying its economic landscape. This transition, at the heart of Vision 2030, is yielding tangible results. The non-oil sector stands as a testament to this commitment, showcasing robust growth. In FY2023, it surged forward at a remarkable 3.8%, painting a clear picture of a vibrant, multifaceted economy taking shape.

This momentum is driven by a confluence of factors: burgeoning private consumption, strategic non-oil investment, and a flourishing tourism sector. Let's delve into the heart of these driving forces:

1. Private Consumption: A Symphony of Economic Confidence

The crescendo of private consumption resonates with the growing confidence in the Saudi economy. This confidence is built on a foundation of positive change:

Job Creation: The Saudi labor market is experiencing a wave of job creation, particularly in the private sector. Unemployment rates are receding, leading to higher disposable incomes and invigorating consumer spending.

Government Reforms: Proactive fiscal reforms and a streamlined business environment have fostered a welcoming space for private sector activity, leading to increased investment and job creation.

Social Programs: Targeted initiatives, like the Citizen Account Program, provide a safety net for vulnerable households, supporting consumption and mitigating the impact of economic fluctuations.

2. Non-Oil Investment: Sowing the Seeds for a Future Harvest

Strategic investment in sectors beyond oil is another cornerstone of Saudi Arabia's diversification success story. The Kingdom is channelling significant resources into infrastructure, technology, and human capital development – the very bedrock of sustained economic growth. Here are some key investment areas:

Infrastructure Development: Mega-projects such as NEOM, Roshn, and the Red Sea Global are driving massive investments in infrastructure, creating futuristic cities, modern housing developments, and captivating tourist destinations. These endeavours attract international businesses and generate new jobs, further propelling economic growth.

Technology and Innovation: Saudi Arabia is on a mission to become a regional powerhouse for technology and entrepreneurship. Investments in artificial intelligence, cloud computing, and cybersecurity, coupled with initiatives fostering a vibrant startup ecosystem, are shaping this exciting landscape.

Human Capital Development: Recognizing that a skilled workforce is paramount, Saudi Arabia is investing heavily in education and training programs. These initiatives aim to equip its citizens with the skills needed for the jobs of tomorrow, including a focus on STEM education, vocational training, and fostering an entrepreneurial spirit.

3.   Tourism: A Rising Star Illuminating the Economic Sky

The Saudi tourism sector is experiencing an unprecedented boom, fuelled by a strategic blend of initiatives:

Easing of Visa Restrictions: The introduction of tourist e-visas has removed barriers for international travellers, significantly boosting tourism inflows.

Development of New Destinations: Mega-projects like the Red Sea Global and Qiddiya are giving rise to world-class tourist destinations, attracting visitors from across the globe.

Promotion of Cultural Heritage: Saudi Arabia is showcasing its rich cultural tapestry, inviting the world to experience its ancient cities, historical sites, and traditional arts and crafts. This initiative attracts cultural tourists and broadens the appeal of the tourism sector beyond religious tourism.

The tourism sector's contribution to GDP reached an impressive 11.5% in 2023, and the IMF forecasts continued growth in the coming years. This surge is generating new jobs, stimulating service sector activity, and contributing significantly to the diversification of the Saudi economy.

The Outlook: Gazing into its crystal ball, sees a future where Saudi Arabia's non-oil sector continues its upward trajectory, forecasting a steady ascent of 3.9-4.4% growth over the medium term. This optimistic projection is fuelled by the twin engines of the ambitious National Investment Strategy (NIS) and the ongoing rise of awe-inspiring mega-projects. However, the report cautions that this journey towards prosperity requires a steady hand on the tiller of reform. Fiscal prudence and continued structural reforms are paramount, ensuring that growth is not only sustained but also shared by all, weaving a tapestry of inclusive prosperity.

Saudi Arabia's metamorphosis away from its reliance on oil is well underway. The non-oil sector, a vibrant butterfly emerging from its cocoon, is demonstrating remarkable resilience and the potential to soar to new heights. The Kingdom's unwavering commitment to nurturing this transformation through investments in infrastructure, technology, human capital, and tourism is laying the groundwork for a dynamic and diversified economy. This positive outlook serves as a resounding endorsement of these efforts, illuminating a path towards continued economic transformation in the years to come.

Giga-Projects: Architecting Saudi Arabia's Ambitious Transformation

Imagine a canvas so vast, it stretches beyond the horizon, ready to be painted with the colours of innovation and ambition. This is the scale of Saudi Arabia's commitment to "giga-projects" – colossal undertakings that form the cornerstone of its Vision 2030 plan. Spearheaded by the Public Investment Fund (PIF) and its treasure chest overflowing with assets exceeding $925 billion, these ambitious endeavours are not merely reshaping the Kingdom's physical landscape, but also sculpting a multi-billion-dollar opportunity for international businesses across a spectrum of sectors.

These giga-projects are not about erecting monuments of steel and glass; they are about cultivating entire ecosystems designed to nourish a diversified economy, attract foreign investment like moths to a brilliant light, spark a wave of job creation, and elevate the quality of life for all Saudi citizens. Let's embark on a journey to explore some of these awe-inspiring projects and the boundless opportunities they unlock:

1.　NEOM: A Beacon of Innovation Rising from the Desert Sands

Envision a city born from the desert, not bound by tradition, but fuelled by the boundless energy of innovation and technology. This is NEOM, a $500 billion testament to human ambition, envisioned as a global oasis for innovation and technology. Sprawling across 26,500 square kilometres, NEOM is designed to be a living laboratory where cutting-edge technologies intertwine with sustainable living and the boundless potential of advanced industries.

Opportunities Abound: NEOM extends an open invitation to businesses across a multitude of sectors, offering a landscape brimming with possibilities:

Construction and Engineering: Building a city from the ground up requires a symphony of expertise, from the grand orchestra of infrastructure development to the intricate melodies of sustainable building practices.

Technology and Innovation: NEOM is a fertile breeding ground for technological advancements, beckoning companies specializing in artificial intelligence, robotics, renewable energy, and the intricate dance of smart city solutions.

Logistics and Transportation: Strategically positioned and pulsating with advanced transportation systems, NEOM opens doors for logistics providers, transportation companies, and manufacturers seeking a hub at the crossroads of the world.

Tourism and Hospitality: NEOM is poised to become a magnet for global tourism, captivating visitors with its futuristic allure, sustainable havens, and a tapestry of unique experiences unlike any other.

2. Roshn: Nurturing Communities, Cultivating Dreams

Imagine a constellation of thriving communities, where modern living harmonizes with Saudi heritage, and the dream of homeownership becomes a reality for many. This is the vision behind Roshn, a large-scale residential housing project designed to address the Kingdom's growing housing needs while fostering a culture of homeownership. Roshn is cultivating integrated communities that offer a rich tapestry of housing options, amenities, and services, catering to a vibrant mosaic of income levels and lifestyles.

Opportunities Blossom: Roshn extends a welcoming hand to businesses seeking fertile ground for growth, offering a landscape ripe with potential:

Residential Construction: The creation of thousands of new homes calls for the artistry of skilled hands in residential construction, the sourcing of high-quality building materials, and the inspired touch of interior design.

Real Estate Development and Management: Roshn's integrated communities require the expertise of those well-versed in the art of real estate development, the delicate balance of property management, and the essential provision of community services.

Retail and Hospitality: Within Roshn's bustling communities, retail spaces will bloom, restaurants will tantalize taste buds, and entertainment venues will come alive, creating a symphony of opportunities for businesses in these sectors.

3. Diriyah Gate: Where History Whispers and the Future Unfolds

Step back in time to Diriyah, the birthplace of the first Saudi state, where echoes of the past are being meticulously preserved and woven into a tapestry of cultural renaissance. Diriyah Gate, a $20 billion testament to Saudi Arabia's reverence for its heritage, is breathing new life into this historical gem, transforming it into a world-class cultural and heritage destination.

Opportunities Unearthed: Diriyah Gate extends a beckoning hand to companies who understand the language of history and possess the skills to revive its grandeur:

Heritage Restoration and Conservation: The restoration of Diriyah's architectural treasures demands a delicate touch – expertise in heritage conservation, the mastery of architectural restoration, and a deep respect for traditional building techniques.

Cultural Tourism and Hospitality: Diriyah Gate, poised to become a global magnet for cultural tourism, will captivate visitors with its captivating museums, vibrant cultural centers, and the bustling energy of traditional souks. This transformation translates into a wealth of opportunities for hotels, restaurants, tour operators, and those who orchestrate unforgettable cultural events..

4. Red Sea Global: Where Azure Waters Embrace Sustainable Luxury

Imagine a constellation of pristine islands, their shores caressed by the shimmering turquoise waters of the Red Sea, where luxury whispers on the breeze and sustainability is woven into the very fabric of existence. This is the allure of Red Sea Global, a sanctuary for discerning travelers seeking an unparalleled escape. Spanning a breathtaking 28,000 square kilometers along Saudi Arabia's Red Sea coast, this ambitious project transcends the traditional boundaries of luxury tourism, offering a symphony of unforgettable experiences while safeguarding the natural wonders that make it so unique.

Opportunities Shimmer Like Pearls Beneath the Waves:

Luxury Hospitality and Resort Development: The creation of opulent havens – from intimate boutique hotels to sprawling resorts and secluded private villas – demands the artistry of skilled architects, the inspired touch of interior designers, and the expertise of construction companies dedicated to crafting masterpieces. Luxury brands seeking to establish a coveted presence in this exclusive paradise will find fertile ground for growth.

Sustainable Tourism and Environmental Management: Red Sea Global is a testament to the power of harmonizing human ambition with the preservation of nature's delicate balance. This commitment opens doors for companies specializing in environmental management, harnessing the power of renewable energy, and implementing eco-friendly tourism practices. Expertise in waste management, water conservation, biodiversity protection, and the development of sustainable infrastructure is paramount.

Marine and Coastal Tourism: The Red Sea, a vibrant underwater kingdom teeming with a kaleidoscope of marine life and breathtaking coral reefs, beckons to adventurers and explorers. Dive operators, boat tour companies, and marine conservation organizations will find a wealth of opportunities to share the wonders of this underwater paradise while safeguarding its future for generations to come.

Adventure and Experiential Tourism: For those who yearn to explore beyond the pristine beaches, Red Sea Global offers a thrilling tapestry of adventure and experiential tourism. Picture exhilarating desert safaris, invigorating hikes through captivating landscapes, and immersive cultural excursions that reveal the heart and soul of the region. Tour operators, adventure tourism companies, and cultural heritage organizations will play a vital role in crafting these unforgettable experiences.

5. Qiddiya: Where Entertainment, Sports, and Culture Converge

Just outside the bustling metropolis of Riyadh, a new landscape of leisure and entertainment is taking shape. Qiddiya, an $8 billion entertainment, sports, and cultural hub, is poised to become a global destination, drawing thrill-seekers, sports enthusiasts, and cultural connoisseurs. Imagine a world-class theme park, a sprawling water park where laughter echoes on the breeze, state-of-the-art sports facilities, and cultural venues that ignite the imagination. Qiddiya promises an escape from the ordinary, a symphony of experiences for every taste and passion.

Opportunities Take Center Stage:

Theme Park and Entertainment: Qiddiya's theme park and entertainment venues will transport visitors to realms of imagination and wonder. This ambitious undertaking requires the expertise of master storytellers – theme park designers, ride engineers, entertainment production companies, and hospitality management groups dedicated to creating seamless and unforgettable experiences.

Sports and Recreation: Qiddiya's state-of-the-art sports facilities – from a heart-pounding motorsports track to a meticulously manicured golf course and an equestrian center where grace and power intertwine – create a haven for athletes and enthusiasts alike. Sports equipment manufacturers, event organizers, and sports training academies will find a receptive audience eager to embrace the thrill of competition and the pursuit of athletic excellence.

Cultural and Performing Arts: Qiddiya's cultural venues, including a world-class performing arts center and a captivating museum, will become a beacon for artistic expression and cultural exchange. Cultural organizations, event promoters, and talented artists from around the globe will find a platform to showcase their craft and inspire audiences.

Hospitality and Retail: No world-class destination is complete without a symphony of culinary delights, retail therapy, and luxurious accommodations. Qiddiya's hotels, restaurants, and retail outlets present a wealth of opportunities for hospitality providers, restaurateurs, and retailers seeking to cater to a diverse and international clientele..

These awe-inspiring giga-projects, along with other transformative endeavors like the verdant oasis of King Salman Park and the ultra-luxury haven of Amaala, are painting a bold new future for Saudi Arabia. The Kingdom is rapidly emerging as a global hub for investment, innovation, and tourism, offering a vast canvas of opportunities for international businesses eager to play a part in this extraordinary transformation. By leveraging their expertise, embracing collaboration, and forging strong partnerships with local stakeholders, businesses can contribute to the kingdom's growth.

Navigating the Fiscal Seas: Charting a Course Toward Sustainability

While the winds of Vision 2030 propel Saudi Arabia towards a future brimming with promise, the IMF report reminds us that even the most ambitious voyages require careful navigation of the fiscal seas. The Kingdom's return to a budget deficit in FY2023, a consequence of fluctuating oil revenues and increased expenditures on transformative projects, underscores the need for a steady hand on the tiller of fiscal management. However, the government is rising to the challenge, charting a course that balances the pursuit of ambitious growth with the imperative of long-term fiscal sustainability.

1. **Fiscal Consolidation: A Gradual Approach to Sustainable Shores**

A steady tightening of the fiscal reins over the medium term is expected, a necessary course correction to ensure the long-term health of public finances. But this is not a call for austerity measures that could stifle growth. Instead, it's about a gradual and measured approach, prioritizing spending efficiency and identifying areas where savings can be achieved without compromising economic momentum or the well-being of Saudi citizens. This will push the kingdom to Steer towards efficiency:

Wage Bill Optimization: The government is addressing the significant portion of spending allocated to the wage bill through a multi-pronged approach. Civil service reform, natural attrition, and a shift towards performance-based compensation are key elements of this strategy. Further fine-tuning, including benchmarking public sector wages against private sector levels to address wage disparities.

Subsidies: Striking a Balance: Fuel subsidies, while playing a vital role in social welfare, represent a significant weight on the fiscal ship. The government has taken commendable steps to streamline these subsidies. It is recommended to have further exploration, including a gradual lifting of the cap on gasoline prices while implementing targeted social programs to provide a safety net for vulnerable households.

Public Investment Management: Investing Wisely: Ensuring that every riyal invested by the government generates a significant return and contributes to the engine of economic growth is paramount. Enhancing project appraisal and selection processes, implementing rigorous cost controls, and fostering a culture of transparency and accountability in all public investment projects are recommended.

The IMF emphasizes that the sequencing of fiscal consolidation measures is not merely a technical detail but a crucial element of success. A hasty approach could inadvertently undermine the very economic growth these measures are designed to safeguard. The report recommends prioritizing non-oil revenue mobilization and targeted spending rationalization over drastic cuts in capital spending, which could have unintended consequences on long-term growth prospects.

2. Revenue Mobilization: Diversifying the Streams of Prosperity

Reducing reliance on oil revenue is not just an economic imperative; it's about building a future where prosperity flows from a diversified and sustainable economic landscape. The government is actively exploring innovative avenues to enhance revenue mobilization, ensuring that the journey towards Vision 2030 is fuelled by a diverse range of resources:

Introducing New Avenues of Revenue: A strategic expansion of the revenue base by introducing a property tax and a personal income tax is critical. These measures, commonly employed by nations around the world, have the potential to generate significant revenue while broadening the tax base and reducing dependence on the ebb and flow of oil income.

Refining Existing Tax Structures: The government is committed to refining existing tax structures, including expat levies, excise taxes, and corporate taxes, to optimize their efficiency and revenue-generating potential. This involves addressing any gaps in VAT policy and carefully reviewing tax incentives to ensure they are effective and aligned with broader economic goals.

Enhancing Tax Administration: A robust and efficient tax administration system is the cornerstone of a fair and equitable revenue system. Strengthening tax compliance, streamlining often-cumbersome tax procedures, and leveraging the power of technology to enhance tax collection processes are all paramount.

3. Strengthening Fiscal Institutions: Pillars of Transparency and Accountability

Building a robust and sustainable fiscal future requires more than just sound policies; it demands strong and resilient fiscal institutions. The government is taking decisive steps to fortify these pillars of transparency and accountability, ensuring that the journey toward Vision 2030 is guided by prudent and far-sighted decision-making:

Crafting a Medium-Term Fiscal Framework (MTFF): The MTFF will serve as a compass, providing a clear multi-year perspective on fiscal policy. This framework will outline revenue and spending plans, define deficit targets, and establish a fiscal anchor to guide policy decisions, fostering transparency, accountability, and strategic long-term fiscal planning.

Enhancing Fiscal Risk Management: The government is weaving a comprehensive fiscal risk management framework to identify, assess, and navigate potential fiscal storms, including those arising from oil price volatility, contingent liabilities, and public-private partnerships. This proactive approach strengthens the government's ability to mitigate risks and ensure the long-term sustainability of public finances.

Operationalizing a Fiscal Rule: To delink government spending from the unpredictable waves of oil price fluctuations, efforts are underway to operationalize a robust fiscal rule. This stabilizing force will help to smooth government spending over time, reducing procyclicality and bolstering fiscal sustainability. The IMF recommends an expenditure rule that integrates a ceiling on expenditure growth and a target for the Central Government Net Financial Assets (CGNFA).

Saudi Arabia's fiscal landscape is undergoing a remarkable transformation, a testament to the Kingdom's unwavering commitment to balancing ambitious growth aspirations with the imperative of long-term fiscal responsibility. While acknowledging the inevitable complexities of such an endeavor, we can picture a government resolutely confronting these challenges head-on. Through a potent combination of fiscal consolidation, strategic revenue mobilization, and the strengthening of vital institutions, Saudi Arabia is charting a course towards a brighter and more sustainable future.

These measures are not merely about achieving a balanced budget; they are about building a more resilient, diversified, and vibrant economy, one that can weather the inevitable storms of global economic uncertainty and fluctuations in oil prices. By demonstrating an unwavering commitment to fiscal responsibility, transparency, and good governance, the government aims to cultivate investor confidence, attract foreign capital, and ensure that the fruits of economic growth are shared equitably among all citizens, now and for generations to come.

While the path ahead will undoubtedly present its share of challenges, demanding adaptability, careful calibration of policies, and an unwavering commitment to reform, Saudi Arabia is on the right trajectory. The Kingdom is laying a solid foundation for a future defined by fiscal soundness, sustainability, and shared prosperity.

A Welcoming Oasis for Investment: Saudi Arabia Extends an Open Hand to the World

Recognizing that foreign investment is the lifeblood of economic diversification and the realization of Vision 2030's ambitious goals, Saudi Arabia is rolling out the red carpet for investors from around the globe. This welcoming embrace is reflected in the Kingdom's steady ascent in the IMD's World Competitiveness Index — a testament to its unwavering commitment to creating a business environment where innovation and opportunity flourish.

1. **Business-Friendly Reforms: Paving the Way for Seamless Investment**

Like a master architect meticulously removing barriers to entry, the government has implemented a series of business-friendly reforms designed to streamline regulations and make it easier for businesses to thrive. These initiatives are transforming the investment landscape, turning challenges into stepping stones on the path to success:

Streamlined Regulations: Bureaucracy, once a formidable obstacle, is being dismantled and replaced by a more streamlined and efficient regulatory environment across various sectors. Businesses now enjoy a smoother path to obtaining licenses and permits. The introduction of the new law on civil transactions, for instance, provides much-needed clarity and predictability in contract enforcement, financial transactions, and the protection of property rights.

Reduced Bureaucracy: Gone are the days of navigating a labyrinthine bureaucracy. The government has embraced the power of digitalization, bringing many government services online and making it easier than ever for businesses to interact with government agencies. This digital transformation is saving businesses valuable time and resources, allowing them to focus on what matters most – growth and innovation. The Etimad platform, for example, has significantly reduced payment delays for private sector contractors, injecting much-needed efficiency into the system.

Improved Access to Land and Financing: Recognizing that access to land and capital are the lifeblood of any business, the government is taking proactive steps to improve access to land for industrial and commercial development. At the same time, efforts are underway to expand access to finance for businesses of all sizes, with a particular focus on empowering small and medium-sized enterprises (SMEs) – the engines of innovation and job creation.

2. **Regional Headquarters Program: Attracting Global Titans to a Land of Opportunity**

Saudi Arabia's ambition extends beyond attracting individual businesses; it aims to become a global hub for multinational corporations. The Regional Headquarters Program is a testament to this vision, a strategic initiative designed to entice global players to establish their regional headquarters within the Kingdom's borders. This program is a symphony of incentives, each note carefully orchestrated to create an irresistible harmony for businesses seeking a strategic foothold in the region:

Tax Benefits: Companies choosing to establish their regional headquarters in Saudi Arabia are welcomed with open arms and a host of tax incentives. These include attractive reductions in corporate income tax rates and exemptions from certain taxes, allowing businesses to reinvest more of their hard-earned profits into growth and expansion.

Regulatory Flexibility: Recognizing that agility and adaptability are crucial in today's dynamic business environment, regional headquarters enjoy a greater degree of regulatory flexibility. This includes exemptions from certain Saudization requirements, allowing businesses to attract and retain top talent from around the world.

Access to a World-Class Talent Pool: Saudi Arabia is home to a young, vibrant, and increasingly skilled workforce, particularly in sectors like technology and finance. This burgeoning talent pool, eager to contribute to the Kingdom's ambitious transformation, is a magnet for multinational companies seeking a competitive edge in the global marketplace

3. Special Economic Zones (SEZs): Cultivating Growth in Targeted Sectors

Imagine fertile grounds where innovation flourishes, and businesses are nurtured with a unique blend of incentives and advantages. This is the essence of Saudi Arabia's Special Economic Zones (SEZs) – designated areas strategically crafted to attract foreign investment and stimulate economic activity in targeted sectors. Each SEZ offers a unique flavor of opportunity:

Tax Advantages: Businesses operating within these vibrant SEZs enjoy a welcoming respite from the usual tax burdens. Reduced corporate income tax rates, exemptions from import duties, and generous tax holidays allow businesses to reinvest more of their hard-earned profits into research, expansion, and innovation.

Regulatory Flexibility: SEZs operate with a refreshing degree of regulatory agility, offering exemptions from certain labor laws and Saudization requirements. This flexibility allows businesses to attract and retain top global talent, fostering a dynamic and internationally competitive workforce.

World-Class Infrastructure and Logistics: SEZs are meticulously designed to facilitate seamless operations and global connectivity. State-of-the-art infrastructure and world-class logistics facilities streamline the movement of goods and services, connecting businesses to the world with ease.

4. Opportunities Abound: Riding the Wave of Transformation

Saudi Arabia's ambitious economic transformation is not just about numbers on a balance sheet; it's about creating a dynamic ecosystem where businesses of all sizes can thrive and contribute to a shared future of prosperity. Key opportunities are emerging across a range of exciting sectors:

Digitalization: Saudi Arabia is a trailblazer in the digital realm, boasting a rapidly expanding digital economy and a vibrant fintech ecosystem. This digital revolution is creating fertile ground for companies specializing in cutting-edge digital services, the ever-expanding world of e-commerce, the dynamic landscape of fintech, and the transformative power of artificial intelligence.

Renewable Energy: The Kingdom is deeply committed to forging a sustainable future, with an ambitious goal of achieving net-zero emissions by 2060. This commitment translates into vast opportunities for companies at the forefront of renewable energy solutions, including solar and wind energy, advanced energy storage technologies, and innovations in energy efficiency and green finance.

Financial Services: Saudi Arabia's financial sector is a beacon of stability and strength, characterized by a robust and well-capitalized banking system and a burgeoning fintech ecosystem. Financial institutions and savvy investors are presented with a wealth of opportunities in retail banking, investment banking, asset management, and the ever-evolving world of insurance.

Tourism: With the tourism sector poised to claim a remarkable 16% share of GDP by 2034, opportunities are cascading like a waterfall for tourism operators, hospitality providers, and businesses catering to the needs of travelers. From luxurious escapes to sustainable havens, cultural immersions, and adrenaline-pumping adventures, the canvas of opportunity is vast and inviting.

Saudi Arabia's unwavering dedication to creating a more favorable investment climate is yielding impressive results. Foreign investment is flowing into the Kingdom, attracted by its ambitious vision, proactive reforms, and the promise of a bright and prosperous future. Multinational companies, recognizing the strategic importance of this dynamic market, are establishing a strong presence, laying down roots for long-term growth and collaboration.

By continuing to implement business-friendly reforms, promoting strategic initiatives like the Regional Headquarters Program and the development of thriving SEZs, and capitalizing on the boundless opportunities presented by its economic transformation, Saudi Arabia is cementing its position as a leading destination for foreign investment and a key player on the global economic stage.

Seizing the Future: Targeted Opportunities in Saudi Arabia's Evolving Landscape

Specific sectors are brimming with investment potential. These sectors, meticulously aligned with the Kingdom's strategic priorities under Vision 2030, offer savvy investors a unique opportunity to participate in a dynamic and evolving market poised for significant growth.

1. Digitalization: Riding the Crest of a Technological Wave

Saudi Arabia is not merely embracing digital technologies; it's riding the crest of a digital wave, positioning itself as a regional powerhouse in the digital realm. The Kingdom's remarkable strides in digitalization, creating a fertile ground for investors seeking to capitalize on this transformative trend are noticeable:

Fintech: A Thriving Ecosystem Beckons: Saudi Arabia's fintech ecosystem is buzzing with activity, attracting significant investment and nurturing a new generation of financial innovators. Opportunities abound for companies specializing in cutting-edge payment solutions, accessible lending platforms, innovative insurance products, and sophisticated wealth management tools. The positive impact of SAMA's regulatory sandboxes and strategic partnerships with international fintech companies, fostering a culture of experimentation and accelerating the pace of innovation in this dynamic sector.

Digital Service Providers: Meeting Soaring Demand: The thirst for digital services in Saudi Arabia is insatiable, creating a wave of opportunities for companies providing essential building blocks of the digital economy – from secure and reliable cloud computing services to robust cybersecurity solutions, powerful data analytics tools, and seamless e-commerce platforms. The government's push for efficient and citizen-centric e-government services, coupled with the rapid adoption of digital technologies by businesses of all sizes, is fueling this surge in demand.

Artificial Intelligence (AI): Unlocking the Power of Intelligent Machines: Saudi Arabia recognizes that artificial intelligence is not just a technological advancement but a key that can unlock a future of enhanced productivity, diversified economic growth, and smarter, more efficient public services. Saudi Arabia is strategically positioned in terms of AI readiness, rivalling the capabilities of many high-income countries. This strategic focus on AI translates into exciting opportunities for companies developing AI-powered solutions across a myriad of sectors, including healthcare, education, transportation, and energy.

2. Renewable Energy: Illuminating a Sustainable Path to Energy Security

The Kingdom is unwavering in its commitment to a greener future, setting an ambitious target of achieving net-zero emissions by 2060. This commitment is not just an environmental imperative; it's a catalyst for investment and innovation in the renewable energy sector, as highlighted by the IMF report:

Renewable Energy Projects: Harnessing the Power of Nature: Saudi Arabia's ambitious plans to harness the power of the sun and wind are creating a surge of opportunities for project developers, investors, and technology providers in the renewable energy sector. With a goal of generating 50% of its electricity from renewable sources by 2030, the Kingdom is rapidly expanding its renewable energy capacity, paving the way for a cleaner, more sustainable energy future.

Energy Efficiency Solutions: Maximizing Every Watt: Improving energy efficiency is not just an environmental responsibility; it's a smart economic strategy. Saudi Arabia is embracing this approach, creating a wealth of opportunities for companies providing innovative energy-efficient solutions for buildings, industries, and transportation systems. The Saudi Energy Efficiency Program (SEEP) is playing a key role in driving the adoption of energy-efficient technologies and best practices across various sectors.

Green Finance: Fueling Sustainable Growth: As the global demand for sustainable investments continues to soar, Saudi

Arabia is well-positioned to become a regional hub for green finance. The growth of this sector is providing crucial support for the Kingdom's transition to a more sustainable and diversified economy, creating exciting opportunities for investors in green bonds, sustainable investment funds, and other innovative financial instruments that channel capital towards renewable energy and other impactful green projects. The positive impact of Saudi Arabia's inaugural sovereign green bond issuance is recognizable, a significant milestone in mobilizing private capital for sustainable investments.

3.   Financial Services: A Solid Foundation, Ripe for Innovation

Saudi Arabia's financial services sector stands as a testament to stability and strength, built on the foundation of a robust and well-capitalized banking system. Yet, this is not a sector content to rest on its laurels. Innovation is in the air, fueled by a burgeoning fintech ecosystem and a supportive regulatory environment. This dynamism, highlighting a wealth of opportunities:

Traditional Banking: A Solid Foundation, Ready for Growth: While innovation is reshaping the landscape, traditional banking services remain the bedrock of the financial sector. Saudi Arabia's banking sector offers a wealth of opportunities in retail banking, corporate banking, and investment banking. Further strengthening of the supervisory framework and enhancement of financial safety nets to ensure continued stability and growth is encouraged.

Fintech: Riding the Wave of the Future: Fintech is not merely a buzzword in Saudi Arabia; it's a force reshaping the financial landscape, opening up exciting new frontiers in payments, lending, and wealth management. Continued support for this burgeoning ecosystem, fostering a culture of innovation through regulatory sandboxes and strategic partnerships with international fintech trailblazers is vital.

Islamic Finance: A Global Leader Charts a Course: Saudi Arabia stands tall as a global leader in Islamic finance, offering unique opportunities for investors seeking ethical and sustainable investments. The sector encompasses a wide range of possibilities, from Islamic banking and sukuk (Islamic bonds) to a growing array of other Islamic financial instruments. The importance of ensuring the effective implementation of regulations governing Islamic banking and the prudent management of liquidity risk is paramount.

4.   Tourism: Embarking on a Journey of Exponential Growth

Saudi Arabia's tourism sector is undergoing a breathtaking metamorphosis, fueled by the government's bold ambition to transform the Kingdom into a global tourism powerhouse. The IMF projects a meteoric rise for this sector, predicting it will contribute a staggering 16% to GDP by 2034. This optimism is deeply rooted in a confluence of factors:

Easing the Path for Global Travelers: The introduction of tourist e-visas has been a game-changer, simplifying the process for international travelers and opening the doors to a more diverse and discerning global audience.

Crafting Unforgettable Destinations: Mega-projects like the Red Sea Global, the entertainment haven of Qiddiya, and the ultra-luxurious haven of Amaala are not merely construction projects; they are the realization of a vision – the creation of world-class tourism destinations offering a symphony of experiences. From opulent resorts and heart-pounding adventure activities to captivating cultural attractions and journeys through time at historical sites, Saudi Arabia is crafting a tapestry of unforgettable experiences.

Showcasing a Rich Cultural Heritage: Beyond its modern marvels, Saudi Arabia is a land of ancient history, vibrant traditions, and a captivating cultural heritage. The Kingdom is proactively sharing this rich tapestry with the world, attracting cultural tourists seeking authentic encounters and diversifying its tourism offerings beyond religious tourism.

Opportunities Abound:

- Luxury Hospitality: Crafting Havens of Indulgence: The demand for opulent accommodations and unparalleled service is soaring as Saudi Arabia welcomes a new wave of discerning travelers. The construction and operation of luxury hotels, exclusive resorts, and private villas present a wealth of opportunities for skilled architects, visionary interior designers, meticulous construction companies, and prestigious luxury brands seeking to establish a coveted presence in this burgeoning market.

- Sustainable Tourism: Preserving Paradise for Future Generations: Saudi Arabia is deeply committed to developing its tourism sector in a manner that respects its natural heritage and preserves its beauty for generations to come. This commitment to sustainability opens doors for companies specializing in eco-friendly tourism practices, environmental management, and innovative renewable energy solutions.

- Experiential Tourism: Creating Memories that Last a Lifetime: Saudi Arabia is a land of contrasts – from the vast expanse of the Arabian Desert to the crystal-clear waters of the Red Sea, from bustling cities to ancient historical sites. This diversity offers a rich tapestry of experiences for adventurers, explorers, and cultural enthusiasts alike. Tour operators, adventure tourism companies, and cultural heritage organizations are presented with a unique opportunity to curate unforgettable journeys and create memories that will last a lifetime.

- Tourism Infrastructure: Building the Foundations of Growth: The rapid expansion of the tourism sector requires significant investment in infrastructure to support its continued growth. This includes the development of modern airports, efficient transportation networks, and world-class hospitality facilities. Construction companies, engineering firms, and logistics providers all have a vital role to play in.

Saudi Arabia is no longer just a land of promise; it's a land of opportunity, beckoning investors seeking growth and diversification. The Kingdom's unwavering commitment to economic transformation, evident in its strategic investments in sectors like digitalization, renewable energy, financial services, and tourism, has painted a compelling and attractive landscape for investors worldwide.

By aligning their investments with Saudi Arabia's ambitious vision, investors have the extraordinary opportunity to not only reap the rewards of the Kingdom's remarkable growth but also to play a defining role in shaping a future defined by diversity, sustainability, and global competitiveness. This is not merely about capitalizing on opportunity; it's about becoming a partner in progress, contributing to a future where innovation flourishes, prosperity is shared, and Saudi Arabia takes its rightful place as a driving force in the global economy.

Charting Your Course: A Compass for Investors Navigating the Saudi Arabian Landscape

While the Kingdom extends a hand of welcome, brimming with opportunities, a strategic and informed approach is essential for success. Here's a guide to help you navigate the terrain:

1. **Due Diligence: Charting a Course Through Risks and Rewards**

In the world of investment, knowledge is power. Thorough due diligence is not merely a box to be ticked; it's the foundation upon which sound investment decisions are made. This is particularly true in a market as dynamic as Saudi Arabia's, where transformation is a constant. Investors must meticulously assess both the glimmering opportunities and the potential pitfalls, taking into account the following:

Fiscal Prudence: Saudi Arabia's fiscal challenges, including the recent return to a budget deficit are acknowledged by the government. Savvy investors would be wise to carefully consider the potential ripple effects of these challenges on their chosen projects. Factors to consider include government spending priorities, revenue mobilization strategies, and the long-term sustainability of public finances.

Navigating Global Economic Tides: The global economy is like a vast ocean, with currents that can shift rapidly and unpredictably. Investors must remain vigilant, considering the potential impact of global economic forces on their investments in Saudi Arabia. Key factors to monitor include the volatility of oil prices, the ebb and flow of global trade tensions, and the ever-changing tides of monetary policy set by major central banks.

Sector-Specific Considerations: Every sector has its own unique rhythm and set of challenges. Investors should approach each sector with a discerning eye, conducting thorough research to understand the nuances of the regulatory environment, the competitive landscape, and the long-term growth potential.

2.   Partnerships: The Power of Local Expertise

Venturing into a new market is like embarking on an expedition into uncharted territory. Having a trusted guide can make all the difference. In the context of Saudi Arabia, collaboration with local partners is not merely advantageous; it's essential for navigating the complexities of the market. Local partners offer invaluable insights, cultural understanding, and access to networks that can be instrumental in achieving success:

Navigating the Regulatory Labyrinth: Saudi Arabia's regulatory environment is constantly evolving, presenting both opportunities and complexities. Local partners, well-versed in the intricacies of the regulatory landscape, can guide investors through the process of obtaining necessary licenses and permits, ensuring compliance with local laws and regulations, and avoiding potential pitfalls.

Bridging Cultural Divides: Saudi Arabia has a rich and unique culture, with customs and business etiquette that may differ from other parts of the world. Local partners serve as invaluable cultural interpreters, helping investors navigate cultural sensitivities, build strong and respectful relationships with key stakeholders, and avoid misunderstandings that could hinder progress.

Unlocking Local Networks and Resources: Local partners, deeply embedded in the fabric of the Saudi Arabian market, offer more than just expertise; they provide access. Access to invaluable local networks, trusted suppliers, efficient distributors, and a wealth of other resources that can streamline operations, reduce costs, and accelerate growth.

3. Long-Term Vision: Investing in a Future Beyond Oil

Investors should prioritize projects that resonate with the heartbeat of Vision 2030, aligning with its transformative goals and contributing to a future where Saudi Arabia thrives in a post-oil world. This means focusing on initiatives that:

Fueling the Engines of Diversification: Vision 2030 is a bold declaration of independence – a commitment to breaking free from the shackles of oil dependency and forging a more diversified and resilient economy. Investors should seek out opportunities in sectors that are at the heart of this transformation, such as the dynamism of the technology sector, the allure of tourism, the promise of renewable energy, and the resurgence of manufacturing.

Empowering the Private Sector: The government is actively fostering a vibrant and thriving private sector, recognizing its role as an engine of job creation, innovation, and economic growth. Investors should prioritize projects that contribute to this goal, breathing life into the private sector, fostering a spirit of entrepreneurship, and enhancing the Kingdom's competitiveness on the global stage.

Embracing a Sustainable Future: Sustainability is not just a buzzword in Saudi Arabia; it's a core principle woven into the fabric of Vision 2030. Investors should champion projects that embody this commitment, promoting environmental stewardship, social responsibility, and the highest standards of governance.

Investing in Saudi Arabia is not just about analyzing numbers on a spreadsheet; it's about embracing a vision, becoming part of a transformative journey. Conducting thorough due diligence, forging strong local partnerships, and aligning their investments with the Kingdom's long-term goals, investors can position themselves not just for success, but for significance, playing a meaningful role in shaping a brighter and more prosperous future for Saudi Arabia.

Saudi Arabia's Metamorphosis: A Symphony of Opportunity Beckons Investors

Saudi Arabia, once synonymous with oil wealth, is writing a new chapter in its story – a tale of bold transformation guided by the ambitious aspirations of Vision 2030. This metamorphosis presents a captivating opportunity for investors seeking not just financial returns, but a chance to participate in a journey of unprecedented change, reshaping the Kingdom's economy, its society, and its place on the world stage.

The IMF report provides invaluable insights into this dynamic landscape. It captures the energy of a Kingdom in motion, celebrating the impressive strides made in diversifying the economy, attracting foreign investment, and cultivating a more welcoming business environment. At the same time, it acknowledges the challenges – the need for fiscal prudence, the ongoing pursuit of structural reforms – reminding us that even the most ambitious journeys require careful navigation.

For investors, the message is clear: Saudi Arabia is a land of immense opportunity, but success requires more than just capital; it demands a strategic vision, careful planning, and a commitment to long-term partnerships. The path forward is clear:

- Targeted Investments: Specific sectors ripe] with potential – the dynamism of digitalization, the promise of renewable energy, the stability of financial services, and the allure of tourism – inviting investors to align their ambitions with the Kingdom's strategic priorities.

- The Power of Partnership: Navigating a new landscape is always easier with a trusted guide. Forging strong local partnerships is vital, tapping into the invaluable knowledge, networks, and cultural understanding that local collaborators can provide.

- Navigating Risks and Rewards: The report doesn't shy away from challenges, encouraging investors to embrace a mindset of due diligence, carefully assessing both risks and rewards, and approaching this dynamic market with a balance of ambition and prudence.

Investing in Saudi Arabia is not merely a transaction; it's an opportunity to become part of a transformative narrative, to contribute to something larger than oneself. By aligning their investments with Vision 2030, investors can play a meaningful role in shaping a future where Saudi Arabia stands tall as a beacon of sustainability, economic diversity, and social progress.

The Kingdom's embrace of innovation, technology, and sustainability creates fertile ground for investments that can generate both financial returns and a lasting positive impact on society. With careful planning, strategic partnerships, and a shared vision for a brighter future, investors can unlock the Kingdom's immense potential and forge a path towards shared prosperity for Saudi Arabia and its people.

CHAPTER 2

Qatar: A Desert Bloom in the Economic Galaxy

Qatar captivated the world as the stage for the 2022 FIFA World Cup, yet its aspirations stretch far beyond the roar of the crowds. The nation is on an inspiring journey of economic metamorphosis, and a recent International Monetary Fund (IMF) report paints a vibrant tapestry of its progress. The report illuminates Qatar's robust growth, its strategic dance towards economic diversification, and an investment climate as stable as it is alluring on the global stage. This chapter delves into the heart of the country unearthing the thrilling opportunities blossoming in Qatar's dynamic economy and spotlighting the key sectors poised for a meteoric rise.

Beyond the Barrel: A Symphony of Diversification

While the hydrocarbon sector remains a bedrock of the Qatari economy, the nation is orchestrating a multifaceted diversification strategy. This commitment to expanding the economic horizon is evident across several key landscapes:

1. **Beyond Oil: The Rise of Non-Hydrocarbon Powerhouses**

The contribution of non-hydrocarbon sectors to Qatar's economic expansion is impressive. This growth is not a happy accident but rather the fruit of meticulous policy decisions and strategic investments.

Public Projects: Seeds of Progress: Qatar has channeled significant resources into public projects, particularly the arteries of its infrastructure. This encompasses investments in transportation networks, such as the Doha Metro and Hamad International Airport, as well as projects nurturing healthcare, education, and the vital organs of social services. These investments have not only enriched the lives of residents but have also cultivated an environment as fertile for businesses as it is for investors.

North Field LNG Expansion: A Rising Tide: While technically anchored in the hydrocarbon sector, the construction phase of the North Field LNG expansion project has unleashed a wave of economic activity in non-hydrocarbon domains. This includes a surge in demand for construction materials, logistics services, and a constellation of support industries, creating a ripple effect of growth felt throughout the economy.

2. Tourism: An Oasis of Opportunity

Qatar's tourism sector is undergoing a breathtaking transformation, drawing strength from the legacy of the 2022 World Cup. The nation's masterful hosting of the tournament has significantly amplified its global presence, beckoning a new wave of tourists eager to experience the unique tapestry of Qatar.

World Cup Legacy: Foundations of Experience: The infrastructure meticulously crafted for the World Cup, including its state-of-the-art stadiums, luxurious hotels, and seamless transportation networks, has laid a robust foundation for a thriving tourism sector.

Tourism Initiatives: A Welcoming Embrace: Qatar is actively pursuing initiatives to court visitors, including simplified visa processes, captivating promotional campaigns aimed at key markets, and the creation of new attractions that shimmer with promise.

Post-World Cup Resilience: A Sustained Surge: the remarkable resilience of the tourism sector in the wake of the World Cup is noticeable, with visitor numbers in 2023 eclipsing pre-pandemic levels. This signifies the sustainability of this tourism boom and its vast potential to fuel economic diversification..

3. Third National Development Strategy (NDS3): A Blueprint for a Bold Future

The eagerly anticipated NDS3 is poised to be a transformative force, a maestro orchestrating Qatar's economic diversification efforts. This comprehensive strategy will unfurl a detailed roadmap, guiding the nation's economic metamorphosis in the years to come.

Private Sector Empowerment: Unleashing a Dynamic Force: NDS3 will champion a more vibrant and dynamic private sector, recognizing its vital role as the engine of sustainable economic growth and diversification.

Innovation and Technology: Embracing the Cutting Edge: The strategy will shine a spotlight on fostering innovation and technological advancement, propelling Qatar to the forefront as a regional hub for knowledge-based industries.

Human Capital Development: Cultivating a Skilled Workforce: NDS3 will prioritize the enrichment of human capital, ensuring that Qatar's workforce is equipped with the tools and expertise needed to thrive in a diversified economic landscape.

4. Growth Projections: A Chorus of Optimism

The IMF forecasts a medium-term growth rate averaging around 5.5%, fuelled by the momentum of the North Field expansion and the strategic implementation of NDS3. This robust growth outlook is a resounding testament to the effectiveness of Qatar's diversification symphony and its magnetic pull on foreign investment. The conviction that Qatar is confidently navigating the path toward its diversification aspirations is recognizable.

In conclusion, Qatar's commitment to economic diversification transcends mere words on a page. The nation is taking decisive action, laying the foundation for a more balanced and sustainable economic ecosystem. The IMF report offers a heartening assessment of Qatar's progress, illuminating the immense potential for continued success as it navigates its diversification journey.

North Field Expansion: A Colossus Igniting Growth

The North Field LNG expansion project, an undertaking of unprecedented magnitude, stands as a towering pillar upon which Qatar's future economic prosperity will be built. Set to propel Qatar's LNG production capacity to new heights by 2028, this project represents a multi-billion-dollar constellation of opportunity for international businesses across a diverse spectrum of sectors.

1. **A Mega-Project with Global Reverberations:**

Scale and Scope: A Paradigm Shift: The North Field expansion is not a mere ripple in the water but a seismic shift in the global LNG landscape, poised to solidify Qatar's position as a true titan. This endeavor encompasses the creation of cutting-edge offshore platforms, sophisticated onshore processing facilities, and an intricate network of export infrastructure, demanding a colossal influx of investment and expertise.

Economic Catalyst: Igniting Growth: The sheer scale of this project sends waves of economic energy throughout Qatar, stimulating growth across a multitude of sectors. The demand for construction materials, specialized equipment, intricate logistics solutions, and a constellation of support industries is fueling a surge in economic activity.

2. Opportunities for International Businesses: A Global Stage

Construction and Engineering: A Masterful Collaboration: The construction phase of the North Field expansion unfurls a golden carpet of opportunity for international construction and engineering virtuosos. The project demands mastery in a symphony of specialized areas, including the intricate dance of offshore platform construction, the strategic choreography of pipeline installation, and the creation of complex processing facilities.

Technology and Innovation: A Frontier of Advancement: The expansion project embraces the cutting edge of technology to elevate efficiency, maximize productivity, and minimize its environmental footprint. This creates a fertile ground for technology pioneers, equipment manufacturers, and innovative minds to contribute their expertise and groundbreaking solutions to this monumental project.

Financial Services: Orchestrating Capital Flows: Financing the North Field expansion requires the finesse and expertise of sophisticated financial services, including the strategic deployment of project finance, intricate insurance solutions, and meticulous risk management strategies. International financial institutions and astute investors have a pivotal role to play in orchestrating the project's financial needs.

3. Meeting Global LNG Demand: A Beacon of Energy Security

Increasing Global Demand: Riding the Wave: The expansion arrives at a time when the global thirst for LNG is more pronounced than ever, particularly from the dynamic economies of Asia and Europe. The global shift towards cleaner energy alternatives, intertwined with geopolitical dynamics, has fueled a surge in LNG demand, positioning Qatar to capitalize on this transformative trend.

Securing Long-Term Contracts: A Foundation of Stability: Qatar has proactively secured long-term LNG supply contracts with key customers across Asia and Europe, ensuring a steady and predictable stream of revenue from the North Field expansion. These contracts form a bedrock of stability for Qatar's long-term economic growth.

Strategic Importance: A Global Energy Linchpin: The expansion will not only propel Qatar's economic ascent but also elevate its strategic significance on the world stage as a reliable and steadfast supplier of LNG to global markets. This reinforces Qatar's position as a key player in shaping the global energy landscape.

4.   Elevating Qatar to New Heights of LNG Dominance:

Production Capacity: Unleashing a Torrent of LNG: The North Field expansion will unlock a surge in Qatar's LNG production capacity, etching its name even deeper into the annals of leading LNG exporters. This expanded capacity empowers Qatar to not only meet the burgeoning global appetite for LNG but to maintain its competitive edge in the ever-evolving energy marketplace.

Technological Advancement: Pioneering the Future of LNG: This ambitious project is a crucible of innovation, driving technological advancements that are redefining the LNG sector and burnishing Qatar's reputation as a pioneer in efficiency and ingenuity. This further solidifies Qatar's standing as the LNG supplier of choice for discerning customers worldwide.

Economic Diversification: A Catalyst for Balanced Growth: While the North Field expansion is deeply rooted in the hydrocarbon sector, its impact extends far beyond, sending ripples of growth throughout the broader economic landscape. The project's transformative effects are fostering the expansion of non-hydrocarbon sectors, nurturing the development of a more resilient and multifaceted economy.

In conclusion, the North Field LNG expansion project is more than a mere construction project; it is a bold declaration of Qatar's ambition, a testament to its vision. This transformative undertaking will leave an indelible mark on Qatar's economic trajectory, unlocking a wealth of opportunities for international businesses while simultaneously propelling Qatar's economic diversification and cementing its position as a true titan in the realm of global LNG.

Charting a Course Through the Fiscal Seas

Qatar's steadfast commitment to fiscal prudence is applauded, evident in its impressive track record of consistently achieving significant fiscal and current account surpluses. This fiscal strength stands as a beacon, illuminating the nation's sound economic stewardship and its dedication to responsible spending. However, the report emphasizes that maintaining this disciplined approach is paramount, particularly as Qatar embarks on an ambitious journey of economic transformation. The IMF provides a clear compass, guiding Qatar to navigate the fiscal seas, expertly balancing prudence with the imperative to support diversification and long-term, sustainable growth.

1.　Anchoring Prosperity: Sustained Fiscal Prudence

Permanent Income Hypothesis (PIH): A Guiding North Star: Embracing a fiscal anchor grounded in the principles of the Permanent Income Hypothesis (PIH) is recommended. This principle advocates for a sustainable spending trajectory that aligns with long-term revenue horizons rather than being swayed by the fickle nature of short-term fluctuations in hydrocarbon revenues.

Intergenerational Equity: A Legacy for Future Generations: The PIH framework safeguards intergenerational equity, ensuring that the current bounty of hydrocarbon wealth is managed responsibly to create a lasting legacy for future generations. This safeguards against excessive spending that could deplete precious resources and jeopardize the economic well-being of future Qataris.

Resilience Against External Shocks: Weathering the Storms: Adhering to a PIH-based fiscal anchor strengthens Qatar's ability to weather external shocks, particularly the unpredictable volatility of global energy prices. By adopting a strategy of smoothing spending over time, Qatar can avoid drastic adjustments in response to price fluctuations, ensuring smoother sailing toward economic stability.

Setting Sail: Operationalizing Fiscal Prudence: The report suggests several practical steps to effectively implement fiscal prudence:

Conservative Revenue Projections: Charting a Realistic Course: Basing budget projections on conservative oil and gas price assumptions, steering clear of the allure of overestimating future revenues.

Contingency Planning: Preparing for Unexpected Squalls: Establishing robust contingency plans to navigate potential revenue shortfalls that may arise from unforeseen circumstances.

Fiscal Buffers: A Safe Harbor in Times of Need: Maintaining adequate fiscal reserves to provide a buffer against unexpected shocks, ensuring the ship of fiscal sustainability remains afloat.

2. Revenue Diversification: Expanding the Economic Horizon

Broadening the Revenue Base: Unlocking New Streams of Prosperity: It is of critical importance to diversify Qatar's revenue streams, reducing its reliance on the ebb and flow of hydrocarbon revenues, which are inherently volatile and susceptible to long-term decline as the world sets sail toward cleaner energy sources.

Introducing a Value Added Tax (VAT): A Modern Trade Wind: The report recommends the implementation of a broad-based VAT as a key measure to modernize the nation's tax system and expand its revenue base. A VAT would provide a steady and predictable source of non-hydrocarbon revenue, filling the sails of fiscal sustainability.

Implementation Readiness: Preparing for Smooth Implementation: Qatar's significant progress in laying the groundwork for VAT implementation, including the development of essential administrative infrastructure and a robust legal framework is vital.

Social Impact Mitigation: Navigating the Social Seas: The report wisely suggests that the introduction of VAT be accompanied by measures to mitigate any potential impact on low-income households, such as targeted social safety net programs, ensuring no one is left behind.

Exploring Other Revenue Sources: Discovering New Horizons: Beyond the implementation of VAT, Qatar to embark on a journey of exploration, seeking out other potential sources of non-hydrocarbon revenue, such as property taxes, excise taxes, and environmental levies.

3. Sculpting Efficiency: Optimizing Expenditures for a Vibrant Future

The IMF report champions a strategic approach to expenditure optimization, akin to a master sculptor refining a masterpiece. The focus is on chiseling away inefficiencies, polishing sustainability, and ensuring that spending aligns harmoniously with Qatar's grand vision for economic transformation. This entails a multifaceted approach:

Honing the Edges: Enhancing Spending Efficiency

The report recommends a meticulous examination of government spending, identifying areas where efficiency can be sharpened and cost savings can be unearthed. This involves:

Performance-Based Budgeting: Investing in Results: Embracing a performance-based budgeting philosophy, where budget allocations are intricately linked to specific outcomes and tangible performance targets. This ensures that funding flows towards programs and initiatives that bear fruit, delivering tangible results and advancing national priorities.

Public Procurement Reform: Forging Transparency and Value: Strengthening public procurement processes to ensure transparency, fostering healthy competition, and extracting maximum value from every riyal spent. This entails streamlining procurement procedures, championing open and competitive bidding, and implementing robust monitoring mechanisms to deter corruption and safeguard the efficient utilization of public funds.

Refining the Form: Rationalizing the Public Wage Bill

Recognizing the substantial weight of the public wage bill on government spending, the report recommends measures to ensure its long-term sustainability and enhance its efficiency:

Wage Structure Review: Striking a Balance: Conducting a comprehensive review of the public sector wage structure to ensure it aligns harmoniously with market rates and promotes efficiency. This involves benchmarking public sector salaries against comparable positions in the private sector, addressing any disparities, and ensuring that compensation remains competitive while adhering to the principles of fiscal sustainability.

Employment Growth Management: Strategic Talent Allocation: Implementing measured approaches to manage the growth of public sector employment, focusing on bolstering essential services and aligning hiring practices with strategic priorities. This involves prioritizing recruitment in key sectors such as education, healthcare, and technology, while exercising restraint in non-essential areas.

Removing Impediments: Phasing Out Subsidies

Gradual phasing out of remaining subsidies is needed, particularly those related to energy. This strategic manoeuvre would not only alleviate pressure on government spending but also foster a more efficient allocation of resources and incentivize the adoption of cleaner, more sustainable energy sources.

Targeted Approach: Precision in Subsidy Removal: The report emphasizes the importance of a surgical approach to subsidy removal, focusing on those that are most distortive and least beneficial to vulnerable households.

Social Safety Nets: Protecting the Vulnerable: The removal of subsidies should be accompanied by the strengthening of social safety net programs, ensuring that low-income households are shielded from any potential adverse impacts on their living standards.

Communication and Transparency: Building Public Trust: Open communication and transparency are vital to cultivate public understanding and garner support for subsidy reform. This involves clearly articulating the rationale behind subsidy removal, elucidating the benefits of reform, and transparently outlining the measures being taken to mitigate any unintended social consequences.

Investing in the Future: Reorienting Spending Towards Growth

Redirecting government spending towards reforms that catalyze private sector-led growth and accelerate economic diversification is recommended. This entails making strategic investments in:

Human Capital Development: Nurturing a Skilled Workforce: Prioritizing education, training, and skills development is paramount to cultivating a highly skilled and adaptable workforce, equipped to drive innovation, enhance productivity, and thrive in a diversified economic landscape.

Research and Development: Seeding Innovation: Investing in research and development is akin to planting seeds of innovation, fostering technological advancement, and nurturing the growth of new industries. This enhances Qatar's competitiveness on the global stage.

Infrastructure: Building Pathways to Prosperity: Targeted infrastructure investments, particularly in transportation, logistics, and digital connectivity, act as arteries of economic growth. They enhance productivity, reduce business costs, and attract foreign investment.

Business Environment Reforms: Cultivating a Fertile Ground for Growth: Streamlining regulations, simplifying the process of doing business, and promoting healthy competition creates a fertile environment where the private sector can flourish and investment can take root. .

By embracing a strategic and forward-looking approach to expenditure optimization, Qatar can ensure that its fiscal resources are deployed effectively. This will support its ambitious economic transformation, enhance long-term sustainability, and pave the way for a prosperous future for generations to come.

A Haven for Capital: Qatar's Magnetism for Investment

Qatar stands as a beacon for foreign investors, a land of opportunity where capital can be deployed in a stable and secure environment. The nation's allure stems from a harmonious convergence of factors, including its robust economic foundations, wise policymaking, and a forward-looking approach to structural reforms. The strides made in fostering labor market flexibility, cultivating a more fertile business environment, and championing digital transformation are impressive – all of which solidify Qatar's position as an investment destination of choice.

1. **Unshakable Foundations: Strong & Resilient Macroeconomic Fundamentals**

Fiscal Strength: A Bedrock of Stability: Qatar's consistent fiscal surpluses, a testament to its prudent spending and unwavering commitment to long-term sustainability, provide an unshakeable foundation for economic stability. This fiscal strength mitigates the risk of sovereign debt distress and cultivates a predictable and secure environment where businesses can thrive.

External Stability: Weathering Global Currents: Qatar's substantial current account surpluses, fueled by robust hydrocarbon exports and a burgeoning non-hydrocarbon sector, contribute to its robust external position. This economic resilience acts as a buffer against external shocks, further bolstering investor confidence.

Stable Currency: A Steady Hand: The Qatari Riyal's steadfast peg to the US dollar provides a haven of currency stability, effectively reducing exchange rate risk for foreign investors. This predictability enhances Qatar's allure as an investment destination, particularly for long-term projects where stability is paramount.

Low Inflation: A Predictable Path: Qatar's proven ability to maintain low and stable inflation creates a predictable operating environment for businesses and investors. This price stability facilitates more accurate business planning and minimizes uncertainty, fostering an environment conducive to growth.

2. **Open Doors & Fertile Ground: An Attractive Business Environment**

Streamlined Regulations: Navigating with Ease: Qatar has taken significant steps to streamline regulations, clearing away bureaucratic hurdles and making it easier for businesses to flourish. This includes simplifying business registration processes, minimizing the number of permits and licenses required, and enhancing transparency in regulatory frameworks.

Enhanced Administrative Efficiency: The Speed of Business: The government is dedicated to accelerating the pace of business by enhancing administrative efficiency, reducing processing times for applications and approvals, and streamlining the overall ease of doing business. This includes harnessing the power of digital technologies to streamline processes and elevate the quality of service delivery.

Public-Private Partnerships (PPPs): Building Together: Qatar actively fosters public-private partnerships (PPPs), recognizing them as a powerful mechanism to leverage private sector expertise and unlock capital for infrastructure development and other strategic initiatives. This collaborative framework provides a clear and transparent roadmap for successful partnerships between the government and private investors.

Investor Protection: A Foundation of Trust: Qatar boasts a robust legal framework that safeguards the rights of foreign investors, ensuring a level playing field where fairness and transparency prevail. The nation's unwavering commitment to upholding the rule of law fosters an environment of trust and security, giving investors the confidence to put down roots and grow.

3.   A Financial Fortress: Stability and Innovation

Well-Capitalized Banks: Pillars of Financial Strength: Qatar's banking sector stands as a testament to stability, characterized by well-capitalized and highly liquid institutions that inspire confidence in investors. These financial stalwarts boast strong balance sheets, adhere to robust risk management practices, and operate under the watchful eye of the Qatar Central Bank.

Deepening Capital Markets: Unlocking New Avenues of Finance: Qatar is proactively nurturing the growth of its domestic capital markets, creating alternative channels of financing for businesses and investors. This includes initiatives designed to stimulate the issuance of bonds and sukuk, as well as efforts to cultivate a more dynamic and vibrant stock market.

Fintech Innovation: Embracing the Future of Finance: Qatar is riding the wave of fintech innovation, injecting fresh energy and competition into its financial services landscape. The launch of a National Fintech Strategy signals Qatar's commitment to fostering a thriving fintech ecosystem, attracting innovative companies, promoting collaboration, and expanding financial inclusion.

4. A Global Crossroads: Strategic Location & World-Class Infrastructure

Geographic Advantage: At the Heart of Global Trade: Qatar's strategic positioning at the intersection of major trade routes linking Asia, Europe, and Africa makes it a natural hub for regional and international commerce.

World-Class Infrastructure: Seamless Connectivity: Qatar boasts an infrastructure that rivals the best in the world, featuring a modern transportation network, a state-of-the-art airport, and a highly developed logistics sector. These assets facilitate the smooth flow of goods and people, reducing business costs, and enhancing connectivity on a global scale.

Free Trade Zones: Gateways to Opportunity: Qatar has strategically established free trade zones that serve as beacons for foreign investment and catalysts for international trade. These zones offer a compelling combination of tax incentives, streamlined regulations, and other advantages.

A Rising Star: Attracting Global Capital

In conclusion, Qatar's unwavering commitment to cultivating a stable and secure investment climate is evident in its robust macroeconomic fundamentals, its proactive approach to structural reforms, and its ongoing efforts to create a business environment that is as welcoming as it is efficient. Qatar's attractiveness as an investment destination, positioning the nation as a rising star in the global economic firmament.

Opportunities Abound: A Transforming Economy Beckons

Qatar's bold economic transformation agenda, intertwined with its unwavering commitment to sustainability and innovation, presents a constellation of opportunities for foreign investors. Those seeking to capitalize on the nation's dynamic growth trajectory will find fertile ground for investment. Several key sectors ripe with potential, offering promising prospects for those who aspire to contribute to Qatar's enduring prosperity.

1.   **Digitalization: Riding the Wave of Technological Advancement**

Rapid Digital Transformation: A Regional Leader Emerges: Qatar has made remarkable strides in its digital transformation journey, securing its position as a regional frontrunner in digital infrastructure and services. This progress is fueled by a strategic vision to harness the transformative power of technology to propel economic growth, advance social development, and enhance government efficiency.

National Fintech Strategy: Cultivating a Fintech Powerhouse: The launch of a National Fintech Strategy underscores Qatar's commitment to cultivating innovation within its financial services sector. The strategy aims to create a thriving fintech ecosystem, attracting cutting-edge companies, fostering collaboration, and expanding access to financial services for all.

Investment Opportunities: A Ground Floor Opportunity: This dynamic environment presents compelling investment opportunities for a diverse range of players, including fintech companies, digital service providers, technology innovators, and venture capitalists seeking to be part of Qatar's burgeoning fintech landscape.

E-Government Initiatives: Streamlining Governance in the Digital Age: Qatar has implemented comprehensive e-government initiatives designed to streamline government services, enhance transparency, and foster greater citizen engagement. This digitalization drive creates fertile ground for companies specializing in e-government solutions, cybersecurity, and the power of data analytics.

Smart City Development: Building the Cities of Tomorrow: Qatar is investing in the creation of intelligent, interconnected cities, leveraging technology to elevate urban living, promote sustainability, and optimize resource management. This presents significant opportunities for companies at the forefront of smart city technologies, including those specializing in the Internet of Things (IoT), artificial intelligence (AI), and big data analytics.

2. Renewable Energy: Harnessing the Power of a Sustainable Future

Commitment to Climate Action: A Green Horizon Beckons: Qatar has set sail towards a more sustainable future, driven by an unwavering commitment to addressing climate change and embracing cleaner energy sources. This journey is guided by the North Star of the National Environment and Climate Change Strategy, which outlines ambitious goals for reducing greenhouse gas emissions and ushering in an era of renewable energy dominance.

Solar Energy Potential: Basking in the Light of Opportunity: Qatar is bathed in abundant sunlight, making it an ideal location for harnessing the power of the sun through solar energy projects. The government is actively encouraging investment in this radiant sector, offering incentives and fostering a favorable regulatory environment.

Energy Efficiency: Squeezing More from Every Drop: Qatar recognizes the importance of making every watt count. It's actively pursuing energy efficiency enhancements across a spectrum of sectors, including buildings, transportation, and industry. This opens doors for companies specializing in cutting-edge energy efficiency technologies, building retrofits that breathe new life into existing structures, and sustainable transportation solutions.

Green Finance: Fueling a Sustainable Tomorrow: The development of green finance mechanisms will be instrumental in fueling Qatar's journey toward a low-carbon economy. This burgeoning field offers exciting opportunities for financial institutions, forward-thinking investors, and green bond issuers to play a pivotal role in advancing Qatar's sustainability agenda.

3.   Tourism and Hospitality: Extending a Warm Welcome to the World

World Cup Legacy: Building on a Triumphant Stage: The 2022 World Cup was more than a global sporting spectacle; it was a catalyst for transforming Qatar's tourism sector. The event significantly elevated Qatar's profile on the world stage, attracting a new wave of curious travelers eager to experience its unique offerings. The world-class infrastructure developed for the tournament – from state-of-the-art stadiums to luxurious hotels and seamless transportation networks – provides a solid springboard for future growth in the tourism sector.

Tourism Diversification: Unveiling Hidden Gems: Qatar is committed to painting a richer and more diverse tourism landscape, moving beyond traditional attractions to cultivate niche experiences, including cultural immersion, exhilarating sporting events, and captivating eco-adventures. This opens exciting avenues for tourism operators, hospitality providers, and other businesses in the tourism ecosystem to cater to a wider spectrum of traveler interests and passions.

Hospitality Infrastructure: Expanding the Horizon of Luxury: The ongoing expansion of Qatar's hospitality infrastructure is breathtaking in its scope. New hotels, resorts, and entertainment venues are rising, presenting compelling investment opportunities for hotel chains, visionary property developers, and hospitality management companies eager to cater to the world's most discerning travelers.

Regional Tourism Hub: A Gateway to Discovery: Qatar's strategic geographic positioning and world-class airport make it an ideal launchpad for exploring the region's many treasures. This presents lucrative opportunities for tour operators and travel agencies to craft multi-destination itineraries that weave Qatar's unique tapestry of experiences into unforgettable journeys.

4. **Human Capital Development: Nurturing the Seeds of Knowledge**

Skills for a Diversified Economy: Equipping a Future-Ready Workforce: As Qatar charts its course toward a more diversified and knowledge-based economy, strategic investments in human capital development become paramount. It's about equipping Qatar's workforce with the knowledge and skills they need to thrive in this dynamic new landscape.

Education and Training: Shaping the Leaders of Tomorrow: Investment opportunities abound in education and training institutions, particularly those at the forefront of providing specialized programs in high-demand fields like technology, engineering, finance, and tourism.

Skills Development Programs: Bridging the Gap: Companies specializing in skills development and vocational training have a crucial role to play in upskilling and reskilling Qatar's workforce, ensuring they're equipped to meet the evolving demands of a rapidly transforming job market.

Lifelong Learning: Cultivating a Culture of Growth: Fostering a culture that embraces lifelong learning is essential for ensuring that Qatar's workforce remains adaptable, resilient, and competitive amidst the relentless pace of technological advancements and shifting industry needs.

Charting a Course: Key Insights for Investors in Qatar

Qatar's economic metamorphosis presents a captivating siren song for foreign investors, but navigating these waters successfully demands a strategic compass, a spirit of collaboration, and a commitment to the long voyage ahead. The IMF report offers invaluable insights for those seeking to capitalize on Qatar's bright and promising future.

1.   Strategic Alignment: Setting a Course for Success

NDS3 and QNV 2030: Navigating by the Stars: Savvy investors will set their sights on projects and initiatives that align harmoniously with Qatar's National Development Strategy (NDS3) and its overarching National Vision 2030. These guiding documents serve as compasses, illuminating the path toward economic and social progress and revealing the nation's priorities and targeted growth sectors.

Economic Diversification: Embracing a Multifaceted Horizon: Investors seeking to make a lasting impact should prioritize sectors that contribute to Qatar's quest for economic diversification, reducing its reliance on hydrocarbons and cultivating a more balanced and resilient economic ecosystem. Promising sectors include tourism, technology, manufacturing, healthcare, and education – each offering fertile ground for growth.

Private Sector Growth: The Engine of Innovation: Investors should champion investments that fuel the engine of private sector growth, recognizing its vital role in driving innovation, creating jobs, and fostering sustainable economic development. Nurturing small and medium-sized enterprises (SMEs), supporting entrepreneurship, and embracing private sector-led initiatives are key to unlocking this potential.

Sustainability: Investing in a Greener Future: Aligning investments with Qatar's unwavering dedication to sustainability is paramount. Prioritize projects that champion environmental protection, responsible resource management, and the transition to a low-carbon economy. Renewable energy, energy efficiency, green buildings, and sustainable transportation solutions offer pathways to both profit and a healthier planet.

Government Support and Incentives: Benefiting from a Tailwind: By aligning with Qatar's national priorities, investors can unlock a treasure chest of government support, enticing incentives, and a more favorable regulatory environment. The Qatari government is actively rolling out the red carpet for foreign investment in strategic sectors, offering a range of incentives, from tax breaks and subsidized land to streamlined approval processes – all designed to smooth the path to success.

2. Partnership and Collaboration: The Power of Shared Vision

Leveraging Local Expertise: Navigating with a Knowledgeable Crew: Successfully navigating the nuances of the Qatari business environment and regulatory landscape requires a deep understanding of local customs, regulations, and established practices. Partnering with seasoned local companies or individuals with a proven track record can provide invaluable insights, facilitating smoother market entry and enhancing the prospects of investment success.

Building Strong Partnerships: Forging Enduring Bonds: Establishing strong and mutually beneficial partnerships with Qatari stakeholders is not just good practice, it's essential for long-term success. This includes cultivating relationships with government agencies, forging alliances with private sector companies, collaborating with academic institutions, and engaging with civil society organizations.

Knowledge Transfer: Sharing the Gift of Expertise: Partnerships act as conduits for knowledge transfer, enabling the exchange of skills, expertise, and cutting-edge technologies. This exchange of knowledge benefits both foreign investors and their Qatari counterparts, fostering a culture of shared learning and growth.

Joint Ventures: Unlocking Synergies for Success: Joint ventures with Qatari companies can be a strategic masterstroke, providing access to established local markets, robust distribution networks, and invaluable business relationships.

Community Engagement: Building Lasting Connections: Engaging with local communities and developing a deep understanding of their unique needs and priorities is essential for crafting sustainable and socially responsible investments. This includes supporting local initiatives, creating rewarding job opportunities for Qataris, and making meaningful contributions to the nation's social fabric.

3. Long-Term Perspective: Staying the Course for Lasting Rewards

Economic Transformation as a Journey: Embracing the Long View: Qatar's economic transformation is not a sprint, but a marathon – a journey that demands patience, strategic thinking, and a steadfast commitment to the long game. Building a diversified and sustainable economy is a gradual process, and investors must be prepared to embrace a long-term perspective.

Building Trust and Relationships: Sowing the Seeds of Enduring Partnerships: Developing strong, trustworthy relationships with Qatari stakeholders is a journey of its own, requiring time, dedication, and genuine effort. Investors should prioritize building trust, demonstrating an unwavering commitment to Qatar's long-term development, and cultivating mutually beneficial partnerships that stand the test of time.

Adapting to Change: Navigating the Shifting Tides: Qatar's economy is a dynamic force, constantly evolving and adapting to new realities..

In conclusion, Qatar's economic transformation is not merely a wave to ride but a tide to harness – an opportunity for investors to be architects of progress and reap the rewards of a nation charting a bold new course. By embracing Qatar's national priorities, forging enduring partnerships, and adopting a long-term vision, investors can be catalysts for sustainable development and share in the bounty of its promising future.

Chapter Conclusion: Qatar – A Symphony of Progress in the Gulf

Qatar's masterful orchestration of the 2022 FIFA World Cup not only captivated the world but revealed its prowess in executing complex projects on a global stage. Yet, the nation's aspirations soar far beyond the realm of sporting triumphs. Qatar is engaged in a breathtaking symphony of economic transformation, guided by a visionary score that prioritizes diversification, sustainable growth, and the creation of a vibrant ecosystem where businesses and investors thrive.

The nation's unwavering commitment to shedding its reliance on hydrocarbons and embracing a more multifaceted economic landscape is evident in the impressive growth of its non-hydrocarbon sectors. This growth is fueled by strategic investments in the arteries of its infrastructure, the allure of its tourism offerings, and the development of its most valuable asset: its human capital.

The North Field LNG expansion project, while rooted in the hydrocarbon sector, acts as a powerful economic conductor, its ripple effects generating opportunities across a multitude of industries and amplifying growth far beyond its immediate sphere.

Qatar's fiscal prudence, anchored in the principles of the Permanent Income Hypothesis, ensures that the fruits of its prosperity are shared equitably among generations while building resilience against unforeseen economic storms. The government's unwavering focus on revenue diversification, the optimization of its expenditures, and strategic investments in key sectors lay a bedrock of sustainability upon which long-term economic prosperity can be built.

The nation's allure as an investment destination is further amplified by its stable and secure investment climate. Its strong macroeconomic fundamentals, a business-friendly environment that welcomes innovation, and a robust financial sector have captured the attention of the global investment community. Qatar's strategic geographic positioning, coupled with its world-class infrastructure, solidifies its role as a dynamic hub for regional and international trade.

Sectors brimming with potential include the transformative realm of digitalization, the radiant promise of renewable energy, the allure of its expanding tourism landscape, and the enduring value of investing in human capital development. Success in this dynamic environment requires a strategic compass, a collaborative spirit, and an unwavering commitment to the long game.

By embracing the roadmap laid out in NDS3 and QNV 2030, leveraging the insights of local experts, and forging enduring partnerships rooted in trust and shared vision, investors can play a pivotal role in shaping Qatar's sustainable future and reaping the rewards of a nation destined for greatness. Qatar's economic transformation is a testament to the power of visionary leadership, its unwavering dedication to progress, and its unwavering resolve to create a prosperous and diversified economy that will benefit generations to come.

CHAPTER 3

Oman: A Tapestry of Transformation Woven Beyond Oil

Oman is undergoing a vibrant metamorphosis, its economic landscape blossoming with the ambitious hues of Oman Vision 2040. This visionary roadmap charts a course away from oil dependency, leading the Sultanate towards a diversified and sustainable future, ripe with opportunities for astute investors. Echoing the insights from different sources like the International Monetary Fund's (IMF) recent Article IV Consultation report, we uncover the compelling narrative of Oman's evolution and spotlight the promising horizons that beckon.

Beyond the Black Gold: Architecting a Resilient and Multifaceted Economy

While hydrocarbons have long been the bedrock of Oman's economy, the Sultanate is resolutely laying the foundation for a more resilient future, diversifying its economic portfolio. This strategic pivot is evident in the impressive ascent of non-hydrocarbon sectors, now emerging as the driving forces of economic expansion.

Witnessing a resurgence, non-hydrocarbon growth accelerated to 2.1 percent in 2023, propelled by the revitalized agricultural and construction sectors, and buoyed by the robust growth of the services industry. This positive trajectory is no mere ripple; it signifies a deliberate and strategic current towards a more diversified economic model. The IMF projects this non-hydrocarbon growth to stabilize at a steady 4 percent over the medium term, underscoring the sustainability of this transformative journey.

Several key catalysts converge to fuel this impressive growth in non-hydrocarbon sectors:

Global Demand Renaissance: As the global economy awakens from recent turmoil, the demand for Omani exports, particularly in non-hydrocarbon sectors, is poised for a surge. This revitalized demand will invigorate sectors like manufacturing, tourism, and logistics, creating employment opportunities and stimulating economic activity.

Structural Reforms: The Catalyst for Change: Oman is implementing a comprehensive suite of structural reforms, meticulously designed to sharpen competitiveness, enhance the business environment, and attract foreign investment. These reforms are leveling the playing field for businesses, nurturing innovation, and propelling productivity growth. Key initiatives include streamlining regulations, enhancing labor market flexibility, and encouraging private sector participation in strategic sectors.

The Rise of Private Investment: Oman is witnessing an influx of private investment, particularly in non-hydrocarbon sectors. This surge is fueled by a confluence of factors, including the government's unwavering commitment to fostering a favourable investment climate, the allure of attractive investment opportunities, and burgeoning confidence in the long-term prospects of the Omani economy. The Oman Investment Authority (OIA) plays a pivotal role in attracting and facilitating private investment, particularly through its strategic divestment program and its laser focus on developing key sectors, such as renewable energy, tourism, and logistics.

This calculated shift towards a more diversified economy not only fortifies Oman's resilience to the volatility of oil price fluctuations but also cultivates a more dynamic and sustainable economic model. The flourishing growth in non-hydrocarbon sectors is generating new employment opportunities, bolstering incomes, and ultimately, elevating living standards for the Omani people. This remarkable transformation stands as a testament to the government's unwavering dedication to building a brighter future for its citizens and positioning Oman as a beacon of investment and economic opportunity in the region..

Oman's Fiscal Symphony: Orchestrating Sustainability Through Prudence

Oman's unwavering commitment to fiscal discipline is applauded, a melody clearly resonating in the remarkable transformation of its fiscal position. Emerging from years of deficits, Oman orchestrated an impressive surplus of 10.1 percent of GDP in 2022, a testament to its fiscal dexterity. This harmonious trend is projected to continue, with an anticipated surplus of 5.5 percent of GDP in 2023. Such virtuosity underscores the effectiveness of the government's comprehensive fiscal consolidation strategy, a symphony composed of three key movements:

Expenditure Refinement: A Study in Efficiency: The government, with a discerning ear, has taken decisive steps to refine expenditures, prioritizing essential spending, fine-tuning efficiency, and eliminating waste. This meticulous approach has involved a careful examination of spending programs, identifying opportunities for cost savings, and implementing measures to enhance budget transparency and accountability, ensuring every note resonates with responsibility.

Revenue Diversification: Composing a Balanced Score: Recognizing the need to lessen its dependence on the fluctuating rhythms of hydrocarbon revenues, Oman has embarked on a path of revenue diversification. This composition involves expanding the tax base, strengthening tax administration, and exploring new sources of non-hydrocarbon revenue. These efforts not only bolster fiscal resilience but also create a more sustainable and harmonious revenue structure for the long term, ensuring a richer symphony of income streams.

Prudent Debt Management: Conducting a Sustainable Tempo: Oman has skillfully implemented a prudent debt management strategy, aiming to reduce public debt levels and mitigate risks. This measured approach involves prioritizing debt repayment, optimizing debt maturity profiles, and diversifying funding sources, ensuring a sustainable tempo for economic growth. The government's proactive approach to debt management has significantly reduced debt vulnerabilities and bolstered investor confidence, attracting a harmonious chorus of financial backing.

Looking ahead, Oman is not content to rest on its laurels. The government actively seeks further fiscal reforms to solidify these achievements, construct even stronger fiscal buffers, and enhance long-term fiscal sustainability, composing a masterpiece of economic resilience. Key priorities on this reform agenda include:

Modernizing Tax Administration: Expanding the Orchestra of Revenue and Ensuring Harmonious Compliance

A comprehensive tax administration reform plan is underway, focused on modernizing systems, processes, and technology to enhance efficiency, transparency, and taxpayer compliance. This reform is crucial to reducing the tax gap, broadening the tax base, and generating sustainable non-hydrocarbon revenue, inviting new instruments into the orchestra of revenue generation. Key elements of this reform plan include:

Implementing VAT e-invoicing: The introduction of VAT e-invoicing will enhance real-time monitoring of transactions, reducing opportunities for tax evasion, and improving compliance, ensuring every note of revenue is accounted for.

Expanding the Taxpayer Registry: Efforts are underway to expand the taxpayer registry to capture all businesses and individuals liable for taxes, further broadening the tax base and bringing more players into the economic symphony.

Simplifying Tax Filing and Payment Processes: The government is simplifying tax filing and payment processes to reduce compliance costs and encourage voluntary compliance, making it easier for everyone to play their part in the fiscal orchestra.

In addition to strengthening tax administration, Oman is exploring the potential introduction of a personal income tax. This would mark a significant step towards diversifying government revenue streams, reducing reliance on hydrocarbon revenues, and enhancing fiscal resilience, adding a powerful new voice to the symphony of income generation.

Phasing Out Untargeted Subsidies: Conducting a More Efficient and Sustainable Energy Sector

Oman is committed to phasing out untargeted electricity and fuel subsidies, a bold move crucial to promoting efficient resource allocation, reducing fiscal vulnerabilities, and conducting a more sustainable energy sector. This reform is being implemented gradually and strategically, with a focus on mitigating the impact on vulnerable households through targeted social safety net programs, ensuring a harmonious transition for all.

The government is strengthening the social safety net to protect vulnerable households from the impact of subsidy reforms. This includes expanding existing social assistance programs, introducing new targeted programs, and enhancing the effectiveness of delivery mechanisms, composing a safety net that resonates with compassion. These measures will ensure that the benefits of subsidy reforms are shared equitably and that vulnerable households are protected from any adverse impacts, creating a fairer and more inclusive economic composition.

Oman's Fiscal Fortress: Building Transparency, Predictability, and Accountability

Oman is meticulously laying brick by brick a foundation of fiscal strength, enhancing transparency, predictability, and accountability in its fiscal policy. This meticulous construction project involves:

Strengthening the Medium-Term Fiscal Framework (MTFF): A Blueprint for the Future: The government is fortifying its MTFF to provide a clearer and more comprehensive roadmap for fiscal policy over the medium term. This blueprint will enhance fiscal planning, improve coordination across government agencies, and offer greater certainty to investors, attracting them to a landscape of confidence and stability.

Exploring the Adoption of a Fiscal Rule: An Anchor for Stability: Oman is exploring the adoption of a fiscal rule, a steadfast anchor to delink spending from the volatile tides of oil price fluctuations and ensure intergenerational equity. A fiscal rule would provide a clear and transparent framework for fiscal policy, enhance credibility, and promote long-term fiscal sustainability, securing a prosperous future for generations to come.

These diligent efforts to strengthen fiscal frameworks are crucial to bolstering investor confidence, fostering macroeconomic stability, and ensuring that Oman's fiscal position remains an unyielding fortress for generations to come.

An Oasis for Investment: Oman's Alluring Investment Climate

Oman is artfully cultivating an inviting and supportive investment climate, a vibrant oasis attracting foreign direct investment and nurturing a fertile ground for businesses to flourish. The Sultanate's steadfast commitment to sound economic policies, its strategic vision for diversification, and its ongoing efforts to enhance the business environment are bearing fruit. Recent upgrades in sovereign credit ratings, now just a stone's throw from investment grade, stand as a testament to the burgeoning confidence in Oman's economic prospects and its unwavering dedication to cultivating a sustainable and prosperous future.

Oman presents a captivating tapestry of attractive features for investors, establishing itself as a prime destination for those seeking growth and expansion in a stable and promising market.

Business-Friendly Reforms: Paving the Path to Success

Oman has embarked on an ambitious expedition of business-friendly reforms, clearing a path for businesses to operate and thrive. These reforms are laser-focused on streamlining regulations, dismantling bureaucratic hurdles, and enhancing transparency, making it smoother for businesses to navigate the regulatory landscape and focus on growth.

Key reforms shaping this business-friendly terrain include:

New Commercial Companies Law: Planting Seeds for Growth: This law simplifies the process of establishing and operating businesses in Oman, providing greater flexibility and reducing administrative burdens, allowing businesses to sprout and grow with ease.

Foreign Capital Investment Law: Extending a Welcoming Hand: This law encourages foreign investment by providing a clear and transparent framework for foreign investors, guaranteeing equal treatment, and safeguarding their investments, extending a hand of partnership and opportunity.

Streamlined Licensing and Permitting Processes: Removing Roadblocks to Progress: Oman has streamlined licensing and permitting processes, reducing processing times and making it easier for businesses to obtain the necessary approvals to operate, clearing the path for swift progress.

Digitalization of Government Services: Embracing the Digital Age: The government is actively migrating government services online, making it easier for businesses to interact with government agencies and access information online, embracing the efficiency and accessibility of the digital age.

These reforms, interwoven with the government's unwavering commitment to improving the ease of doing business, are transforming Oman into an increasingly attractive destination for both domestic and foreign investors seeking fertile ground for growth.

Enhanced Social Protection: Investing in Human Capital and Cultivating Social Equity

Oman's dedication to building a more inclusive and equitable society is evident in its newly implemented social protection law, a safety net woven with care. This comprehensive law provides a wide array of benefits, strengthening social safety nets, and ensuring a basic level of support for all citizens, nurturing a society where everyone thrives.

Key features of this compassionate legislation include:

Universal Child Benefits: Nurturing the Future: These benefits provide financial support to families with children, helping to reduce child poverty and improve child well-being, investing in a brighter future.

Disability Benefits: Empowering Independence: These benefits provide financial support to individuals with disabilities, enabling them to live with dignity and participate fully in society, fostering a society that embraces inclusivity.

Senior Citizen Benefits: Honouring Experience: These benefits provide financial support to senior citizens, ensuring their financial security and well-being in their later years, honoring their contributions and providing peace of mind.

Harmonized Pension System: A Safety Net for All: The new law harmonizes pension entitlements across public and private sectors, creating a more equitable and sustainable pension system and facilitating greater labor mobility, ensuring a safety net that extends to all.

These social protection measures not only enhance social equity but also contribute to a more productive and stable workforce, benefiting businesses and the economy as a whole, a virtuous cycle of prosperity and well-being.

Improved Governance: A Symphony of Transparency, Accountability, and Efficiency

Oman is orchestrating a harmonious symphony of enhanced governance, transparency, and accountability across all sectors, creating a predictable and reliable concerto for businesses to thrive. The Oman Investment Authority (OIA) takes center stage, conducting this transformation with a keen focus on elevating the governance of state-owned enterprises (SOEs).

The OIA's Rawabet program takes the spotlight, a comprehensive initiative meticulously designed to fine-tune the governance, performance, and risk management within SOEs. Key movements of this transformative composition include:

Robust Code of Governance for SOEs: Setting the Tempo for Integrity: This code establishes a clear rhythm of transparency, accountability, and ethical conduct within SOEs, ensuring every note resonates with integrity.

Performance Assessments: Fine-tuning for Optimal Performance: Regular performance assessments serve as a conductor's baton, monitoring the performance of SOEs and identifying areas for improvement, ensuring a harmonious blend of efficiency and effectiveness.

Risk Management Frameworks: Harmonizing Risk and Opportunity: Comprehensive risk management frameworks provide a safety net, identifying, assessing, and mitigating risks within SOEs, allowing them to confidently navigate the complexities of the economic landscape.

The OIA doesn't stop there, it is actively pursuing a strategic divestment program, gracefully reducing the state's role in the economy and opening up a stage for private investors in sectors previously dominated by SOEs. This strategic maneuver is fostering a more competitive business environment, attracting foreign investment, and composing a vibrant symphony of economic diversification.

A Compelling Investment Overture

These initiatives, harmonizing with Oman's strategic location, abundant natural resources, and skilled workforce, compose a compelling overture for businesses seeking growth and expansion in a stable and promising market. Oman stands as a land of opportunity, its government conducting an orchestra of policies designed to create an environment where businesses can flourish and contribute to the country's sustainable development.

Key Takeaways for Investors: Navigating Oman's Transformative Symphony

Oman's economic transformation under Oman Vision 2040 presents an enthralling symphony of opportunity for investors seeking growth and diversification in a stable and promising market. The Sultanate is not merely fine-tuning its economic model; it is composing a grand and ambitious symphony of transformation, creating a wealth of opportunities for discerning investors who can read the rhythm of this evolving landscape. Here are key takeaways to guide investors as they navigate this exciting composition:

Strategic Alignment: Harmonizing with Oman's Vision for the Future

Oman Vision 2040 is not merely a policy document; it is a masterful score for the Sultanate's future, outlining a clear melody for economic diversification and sustainable development. Investors seeking to maximize their returns and contribute to Oman's long-term success should harmonize their investments with the strategic sectors highlighted in this visionary score.

Key sectors poised for a dramatic crescendo include:

Renewable Energy: A Powerful Chorus of Sustainability: Oman is rapidly emerging as a global virtuoso in green hydrogen production, attracting billions of dollars in foreign investment. Investing in this burgeoning sector offers the potential for high returns while composing a cleaner and more sustainable energy future.

Tourism: Unveiling Oman's Majestic Beauty: Oman's stunning natural beauty, rich cultural heritage, and growing tourism infrastructure make it an alluring stage for tourism-related investments. Opportunities abound in hospitality, travel, leisure, and entertainment, as Oman seeks to attract a larger audience to its captivating performance.

Logistics: Conducting a Global Flow of Goods: Oman's strategic location and its ongoing investments in world-class logistics infrastructure are transforming the Sultanate into a regional logistics maestro. Investing in logistics, transportation, and warehousing offers the potential for significant growth as Oman capitalizes on its strategic position and its expanding trade links with the world.

Manufacturing: Forging a Path to Industrial Harmony: Oman is actively promoting the growth of its manufacturing sector, orchestrating a focus on value-added industries that leverage local resources and expertise. Investing in manufacturing, particularly in sectors like food processing, chemicals, and building materials, offers the potential for strong returns as Oman seeks to become a regional manufacturing powerhouse.

Fisheries: Harvesting the Bounty of the Sea: Oman's rich fishing grounds and its commitment to sustainable fisheries management make it an attractive harbor for fisheries-related investments. Opportunities exist in aquaculture, fish processing, and seafood exports as Oman seeks to maximize the value of its marine resources.

These strategic sectors are not only supported by government initiatives and incentives but also by a growing domestic market, a skilled workforce, and a business-friendly environment, creating a harmonious composition for success. By aligning their investments with Oman Vision 2040, investors can position themselves to capitalize on the Sultanate's long-term growth trajectory, composing a symphony of shared prosperity.

Partnership Opportunities: Unlocking Success with Local Guides

Navigating the uncharted waters of a new market can be a thrilling adventure, and Oman, with its own unique currents, is no exception. Forging alliances with local entities is paramount for investors seeking to navigate these waters successfully and unearth the treasures of the Omani market. Local partners, like seasoned navigators, can provide invaluable insights, helping investors steer clear of obstacles and chart a course toward prosperity.

Key benefits of joining forces with local entities include:

Market Expertise: Unveiling Hidden Treasures: Local partners possess an intimate knowledge of the Omani market, its ebbs and flows, its hidden coves, and its bountiful resources. They can provide invaluable insights into consumer preferences, market trends, and the competitive landscape, revealing the hidden treasures of this dynamic market.

Regulatory Guidance: Navigating the Trade Winds: Navigating the regulatory seas in a new market can be complex and time-consuming, fraught with hidden shoals and unexpected storms. Local partners act as expert navigators, guiding investors through the intricacies of local regulations, ensuring a smooth and efficient entry into the market and avoiding costly delays.

Network Access: Unlocking a Treasure Chest of Connections: Local partners have cultivated a rich network of relationships with key stakeholders, including government agencies, business associations, and potential customers, holding the keys to a treasure chest of connections. This invaluable network can open doors for investors and facilitate fruitful business development, accelerating their journey to success.

Building strong partnerships with local entities can significantly enhance investors' chances of success in the Omani market, mitigating risks and maximizing returns, ensuring a prosperous voyage in these exciting waters.

Long-Term Perspective: Cultivating Enduring Prosperity

Oman's economic transformation is a journey of a thousand leagues, requiring investors to adopt a patient and strategic approach, like master sailors embarking on a long and rewarding voyage. Short-term gains should not overshadow the pursuit of enduring prosperity. Investors should set their sights on establishing businesses that contribute to Oman's long-term development goals, creating lasting value for both their stakeholders and the Omani people, a legacy that will stand the test of time.

Key considerations for this long-term voyage in Oman include:

Sustainability: Charting a Course for Future Generations: Invest in businesses that are environmentally and socially responsible, aligning with Oman's commitment to sustainable development and leaving a positive wake for future generations.

Job Creation: Empowering Local Crews: Prioritize investments that create employment opportunities for Omanis, contributing to the development of a skilled and productive workforce and empowering local communities to thrive.

Knowledge Transfer: Sharing Navigational Expertise: Seek opportunities to share knowledge and expertise with Omani partners, contributing to the development of local capacity and empowering them to navigate their own course toward success.

By adopting a long-term perspective and focusing on cultivating sustainable businesses, investors can create a legacy of enduring prosperity, contribute to Oman's economic transformation, and strengthen their own reputation as responsible and impactful investors, ensuring their voyage in Oman leaves a positive and lasting impact.

Seizing the Opportunity: A New Dawn Beckons in Oman

Oman's economic transformation unfurls like a treasure map, revealing a wealth of opportunities for investors seeking growth and diversification in a stable and promising market. The Sultanate is meticulously crafting a future brimming with prosperity, built on a diversified economy, an unwavering commitment to sustainability, and a welcoming embrace of foreign investment. By aligning their investments with the guiding star of Oman Vision 2040, forging strong partnerships with local guides, and adopting a long-term perspective, investors can expertly navigate the currents of change and capitalize on the exciting opportunities emerging in Oman's dynamic and ever-evolving economy. The message rings clear across the seas: Oman's shores are open for business, and the time to embark on this exciting voyage is now!.

Chapter Conclusion: Oman's Metamorphosis - A Symphony of Opportunity Awaits

This chapter has unveiled the compelling story of Oman's ongoing economic transformation, a vibrant tapestry woven with the threads of Oman Vision 2040. The Sultanate, with unwavering determination, is navigating away from its reliance on hydrocarbons, charting a course towards a diversified, sustainable, and resilient economy, a landscape brimming with potential. This strategic shift is evident in the impressive growth of non-hydrocarbon sectors, fueled by a global resurgence in demand, a symphony of comprehensive structural reforms, and a surge of private investment, breathing new life into the Omani economy.

Oman's steadfast commitment to fiscal discipline deserves a standing ovation. The dramatic transformation from years of deficits to consecutive surpluses showcases the virtuoso performance of the government's fiscal consolidation strategy, a testament to their commitment to sound economic management. Furthermore, the government is orchestrating additional reforms to modernize tax administration, phase out untargeted subsidies, and fortify fiscal frameworks, ensuring a harmonious melody of long-term fiscal sustainability and bolstering investor confidence, attracting a chorus of investment to Oman's shores.

Creating a welcoming investment climate takes center stage in Oman's strategy for attracting foreign direct investment and propelling economic growth. The Sultanate is raising the curtain on business-friendly reforms, strengthening its social safety net, and enhancing governance, creating a fertile ground where businesses can take root and flourish. These initiatives, harmonizing with Oman's strategic location, abundant natural resources, and skilled workforce, compose an irresistible symphony, beckoning investors seeking growth and diversification in a stable and promising market.

For investors, the final curtain reveals a clear message: Oman is a land of boundless opportunity. By aligning their investments with the spotlight of strategic sectors outlined in Oman Vision 2040, forging strong partnerships with local Sherpas, and embracing a long-term perspective, investors can not only capitalize on the Sultanate's transformative journey and contribute to its sustainable development but also reap significant rewards, sharing in the success of this remarkable metamorphosis. The time to invest in Oman is now, as the Sultanate raises the curtain on a new dawn of economic prosperity!

CHAPTER 4

UAE: A Rising Phoenix in the Global Economy

The United Arab Emirates (UAE) is swiftly ascending as a global economic powerhouse, its wings powered by a bold diversification strategy and an unwavering commitment to sustainable growth. This chapter, drawing insights from different sources including the International Monetary Fund's (IMF) June 2023 Article IV Consultation report, embarks on a journey through the UAE's vibrant economic landscape, uncovering both golden opportunities and potential mirages for investors.

Beyond the Black Gold: A Diversification Odyssey

While oil continues to flow through the veins of the UAE's economy, the nation has embarked on a remarkable odyssey of diversification, transforming its landscape into a tapestry of industries. This strategic shift is evident in the projected non-hydrocarbon GDP growth, expected to reach a robust 3.8% in 2023, a testament to the UAE's metamorphosis. Several key winds propel this impressive growth:

Robust Domestic Activity: A Hive of Industry: The UAE's domestic economy is a hive of activity, buzzing with a resurgence in consumer spending and business investment. This revitalization is particularly noticeable in sectors like retail, hospitality, and real estate, where the spirit of innovation and growth is palpable.

Tourism Renaissance: A Phoenix Takes Flight: The tourism sector has experienced a phoenix-like resurgence following the pandemic, soaring beyond expectations. This remarkable comeback is attributed to the UAE's masterful hosting of the Dubai World Expo, an event that captivated millions and showcased the nation's capabilities on a global stage. Moreover, the upcoming FIFA World Cup in neighbouring Qatar is expected to create a ripple effect, further boosting the UAE's tourism industry.

Capital Expenditure: Building a Foundation for the Future: The UAE government continues to invest heavily in infrastructure projects, constructing a solid foundation for the future. These visionary investments, encompassing transportation, logistics, and renewable energy, not only generate employment opportunities and stimulate economic activity but also enhance the UAE's allure as a global business hub.

UAE's 2050 Strategies: A Roadmap to a Sustainable Oasis: The UAE's long-term vision, enshrined in its ambitious 2050 strategies, provides a detailed roadmap for achieving sustainable and diversified growth. These strategies prioritize key sectors such as trade, digitalization, and green initiatives, attracting foreign investment and nurturing a thriving ecosystem of innovation.

The IMF projects that this non-hydrocarbon growth will continue its upward trajectory in the medium term, underpinned by these strategic initiatives and the UAE's unwavering commitment to progress.

Manufacturing: The Engine of Future Growth

The manufacturing sector is poised to become a powerful engine driving future growth in the UAE, fueled by both hydrocarbon and non-hydrocarbon industries. The UAE's strategic focus on developing downstream industries in the hydrocarbon sector, such as petrochemicals and refining, is forging new opportunities for manufacturing to flourish. Additionally, the flourishing growth of non-hydrocarbon sectors like renewable energy, aerospace, and advanced technology is further accelerating the demand for manufacturing activities.

Key Initiatives: Catalysts for Transformation

The UAE's commitment to diversification is evident in its proactive policies and strategic investments, transforming its economic landscape into a vibrant tapestry of opportunity. Key initiatives catalysing this transformation include:

Comprehensive Economic Partnership Agreements (CEPAs): Building Bridges to Global Markets: The UAE is actively pursuing CEPAs with key trading partners worldwide, building bridges to new markets and opportunities. These agreements aim to dismantle trade barriers, boost exports, and attract foreign investment, further diversifying the economy and integrating the UAE into global value chains.

Digitalization: Embracing the Digital Frontier: The UAE is boldly embracing the digital frontier, investing heavily in digital infrastructure and cutting-edge technologies, including artificial intelligence, blockchain, and cloud computing. This digital revolution is unlocking new possibilities for businesses across various sectors, from e-commerce and fintech to healthcare and education.

Green Initiatives: Seeding a Sustainable Future: The UAE is deeply committed to achieving net-zero emissions by 2050, sowing the seeds for a sustainable future. Its substantial investments in renewable energy, green finance, and sustainable infrastructure are not only contributing to global sustainability efforts but also cultivating new economic opportunities in green technologies and industries.

The UAE's dedication to diversification is reshaping its destiny, reducing its dependence on oil and establishing it as a global beacon of innovation, sustainability, and economic dynamism. As the UAE continues to write its success story, the world watches with anticipation, eager to witness the next chapter in this remarkable journey of transformation.

UAE: An Oasis of Innovation and Investment in a Shifting Desert

The UAE has masterfully positioned itself as a global oasis of innovation and investment, a shimmering beacon attracting significant attention from international businesses and investors seeking fertile ground for growth. This magnetic appeal is fueled by a confluence of strategic advantages:

Business-Friendly Reforms: Clearing the Path for Growth: The UAE government has rolled out the red carpet for businesses, implementing a series of reforms that have streamlined regulations, dismantled bureaucratic hurdles, and cultivated a fertile environment for investment to flourish. These reforms have significantly enhanced the ease of doing business in the UAE, transforming it into an irresistible magnet for foreign companies.

Strategic Location: A Crossroads of Opportunity: Nestled at the crossroads of Europe, Asia, and Africa, the UAE occupies an enviable strategic location, a gateway to global commerce. This prime positioning provides businesses with unparalleled access to key markets and trade routes, making it an ideal launchpad for regional and global operations.

World-Class Infrastructure: A Foundation for Excellence: The UAE boasts a foundation of world-class infrastructure, from its modern airports and bustling seaports to its sophisticated telecommunications networks and efficient transportation systems. This robust infrastructure empowers seamless business operations, streamlines logistics, and fosters connectivity, further solidifying the UAE's allure to investors.

Innovation Ecosystem: Nurturing Seeds of Ingenuity: The UAE is actively cultivating a vibrant ecosystem of innovation, investing generously in research and development, nurturing technology incubators, and providing unwavering support to burgeoning start-ups. This unwavering focus on innovation acts as a magnet for entrepreneurs, tech companies, and visionary investors eager to capitalize on the UAE's dynamic and forward-thinking spirit.

Digital and Green Technologies: Pioneering a Sustainable Future: The UAE stands at the forefront of a technological revolution, embracing and investing significantly in digital and green technologies. This includes substantial investments in artificial intelligence, blockchain, renewable energy, and sustainable infrastructure, paving the way for a brighter future. These investments not only contribute to the UAE's own economic diversification but also position it as a global leader in the collective journey toward a more sustainable future.

UAE's remarkable ability to attract safe-haven inflows and orchestrate major Initial Public Offerings (IPOs) is noticeable, even amidst the turbulent winds of global uncertainty. This underscores the unwavering confidence that investors place in the UAE's economic resilience, stability, and promising long-term growth prospects.

Attracting Safe-Haven Inflows: A Beacon of Stability

The UAE has become a sought-after safe haven for investors seeking shelter and security amidst the storms of global economic turbulence. This unwavering appeal stems from a combination of factors:

Stable Political Environment: A Foundation of Confidence: The UAE enjoys a stable political environment, a bedrock of confidence that provides investors with a sense of security and predictability, allowing them to plan for the future with peace of mind.

Strong Economic Fundamentals: Weathering the Storms: The UAE's robust economic fundamentals, built on a diversified economy, a sound fiscal position, and a well-regulated financial system, make it a reliable and attractive harbor for investment, capable of weathering any storm.

Currency Peg to the US Dollar: An Anchor of Stability: The UAE dirham's steadfast peg to the US dollar provides unwavering currency stability, mitigating exchange rate risks for investors and offering a safe haven for their capital.

Successful IPOs: A Rising Tide of Confidence

The UAE has witnessed a wave of successful IPOs in recent years, drawing significant capital from both domestic and international investors eager to ride the wave of its success. This surge in confidence is attributed to:

Growing Investor Confidence: A Testament to Progress: The UAE's impressive economic performance, its business-friendly environment, and its unwavering commitment to innovation have fueled a surge in investor confidence, making IPOs an increasingly attractive proposition.

Supportive Regulatory Framework: Guiding the Way: The UAE provides a well-regulated and transparent capital market, a clear and reliable framework that fosters a conducive environment for successful IPOs.

Strong Demand from Institutional Investors: Seizing the Opportunity: The UAE's IPOs have ignited strong demand from institutional investors, both within the region and globally, as they seek to capitalize on the nation's remarkable growth potential.

The UAE's remarkable success in attracting investment and nurturing innovation is a testament to its strategic vision, its proactive policies, and its unwavering commitment to crafting a sustainable and prosperous future. This potent combination establishes the UAE as an irresistible destination for businesses and investors seeking to seize the opportunities presented by a dynamic and rapidly evolving global economy.

Charting a Course Through the Fiscal Seas

The UAE's fiscal landscape currently radiates strength and stability, a testament to its prudent financial navigation and the favorable winds of elevated oil prices. Robust fiscal vessel, forecasting clear skies and plentiful bounty in the form of large surpluses in the coming years is paramount. The general government fiscal balance is expected to maintain a healthy average of 3.8 percent of GDP over the medium term, a testament to the UAE's seaworthiness. This positive outlook is further buoyed by the UAE's unwavering commitment to maintaining a prudent fiscal course, evident in its successful issuance of USD 7 billion in international bonds and AED 9 billion in domestic bonds, attracting a fleet of investors confident in the UAE's economic voyage.

However, a cautionary flag emphasizes the importance of further reinforcing the UAE's fiscal hull to withstand potential future storms, particularly the unpredictable tides of oil price volatility and the global currents shifting towards a lower-carbon economy. The report outlines key navigational strategies for weathering these potential storms:

1. **Maintaining a Prudent Fiscal Course: Steering Clear of Excess**

Avoiding Procyclical Spending: Resisting the Siren Song of Excess: The UAE should resist the allure of excessive spending during periods of abundant oil revenue, like a wise captain resisting the siren song of extravagance during calm seas. Instead, it should prioritize saving a significant portion of these windfalls to build robust fiscal buffers, providing a cushion against future economic squalls or a drop in oil prices.

Building Fiscal Buffers: Preparing for Stormy Seas: Accumulating fiscal reserves during periods of economic prosperity is akin to stocking the ship's hold for leaner times. These reserves act as a lifeline, providing the means to counter economic downturns, finance strategic investments, or support essential social safety nets when the seas turn rough.

2. **Broadening the Revenue Base: Hoisting the Sails of Diversification**

Enhancing Non-Hydrocarbon Revenue: Catching New Winds of Prosperity: Reducing reliance on oil revenue is crucial for long-term fiscal sustainability, like a skilled sailor harnessing the power of diverse winds to navigate treacherous waters. The UAE should continue to diversify its revenue streams by expanding its non-hydrocarbon revenue base, setting a course for a future less reliant on the unpredictable tides of oil. This can be achieved through strategic maneuvers such as:

Introducing New Taxes: Charting a New Course: The newly introduced corporate income tax (CIT) is a significant step towards broadening the tax base, like adding a new sail to harness the winds of prosperity. It is expected to improve the adjusted non-hydrocarbon primary deficit by 2.2 percentage points to 20.4 percent of non-hydrocarbon GDP over 2023-2027, steering the UAE toward a more diversified economic horizon.

Expanding the Tax Base: Exploring New Horizons: Exploring other potential tax avenues, such as property taxes or value-added taxes, is akin to mapping new trade routes, offering further opportunities to enhance non-hydrocarbon revenue and secure the UAE's fiscal future.

Improving Tax Collection Efficiency: Plugging the Leaks: Strengthening tax administration, leveraging technology to optimize efficiency, and effectively addressing tax evasion can significantly improve revenue collection, preventing valuable resources from slipping through the cracks and ensuring a watertight fiscal vessel.

3. **Improving Expenditure Efficiency: Optimizing for a Smooth Voyage**

Gradual Phase-Out of Subsidies: Adjusting the Rudder: While subsidies can provide social benefits, they can also strain government finances and distort market mechanisms, like an unbalanced load on a ship. The UAE should implement a gradual and well-communicated phase-out of subsidies, like carefully adjusting the rudder, accompanied by targeted measures to mitigate the impact on vulnerable households, ensuring no one is left adrift.

Strengthening Social Safety Nets: Providing a Lifeline: As subsidies are gradually withdrawn, it is crucial to strengthen social safety nets to protect vulnerable populations from potential economic hardship, providing a lifeline for those who need it most. This includes expanding social assistance programs, improving access to healthcare and education, and providing targeted support for low-income households, ensuring that everyone onboard benefits from the UAE's journey toward a more sustainable future.

Growth-Friendly Consolidation: A Steady Course Forward: It is anticipated that a growth-friendly and credible medium-term average annual consolidation of the non-hydrocarbon primary fiscal deficit of around 0.4 percent of non-hydrocarbon GDP, advocating for a steady and sustainable course. This gradual consolidation approach aims to strike a balance between ensuring fiscal sustainability and fostering continued economic growth and development, navigating the UAE toward a brighter and more prosperous future.

4. Fortifying the Nation's Treasury: Building an Impregnable Fortress

The following presents a blueprint for further bolstering the nation's fiscal defences, fortifying its financial fortress to withstand any storm:

Broadening the Tax Base: Expanding the Kingdom's Coffers: Continuously exploring avenues to expand the tax base, whether through the introduction of new levies or extending the reach of existing ones, is akin to discovering new tributaries flowing into the kingdom's coffers, ensuring a steady stream of revenue to fuel its ambitions.

Improving Tax Collection Efficiency: Guarding Against Leakage: Implementing measures to enhance tax compliance, streamline tax administration, and harness the power of technology can significantly bolster revenue collection, preventing leakage and ensuring that every coin rightfully reaches the treasury, strengthening the kingdom's financial foundations.

Containing Expenditure Growth: A Prudent Hand on the Royal Purse: Maintaining a firm grip on government spending, prioritizing essential expenditures, and demanding efficiency in public service delivery are akin to a wise ruler managing the royal purse with prudence, ensuring that resources are allocated wisely and waste is minimized.

Gradually Phasing Out Subsidies: Nurturing Self-Reliance: Continuing the gradual phase-out of subsidies, while providing a safety net for vulnerable groups, is like encouraging a fledgling bird to take flight, gradually reducing dependence while ensuring a safe landing. This approach can lighten the fiscal burden and foster a more dynamic and efficient market, allowing the kingdom's economy to soar to new heights.

By diligently following these recommendations, the UAE can safeguard its fiscal sustainability, enhance its resilience to economic tremors, and lay a solid foundation for achieving its long-term economic aspirations, including its ambitious diversification strategy and its transition toward a more sustainable and radiant future. This proactive approach to fiscal stewardship will not only fortify the UAE's economic foundations but also solidify its position as a global paragon of economic stability and resilience, a beacon of prosperity in an often-uncertain world.

A Financial Citadel: The UAE's Secure and Stable Financial System

The UAE's financial system stands as an impenetrable citadel, a testament to its overall stability and unwavering resilience. Robust health of the UAE's banks is clear, likening them to mighty fortresses, their strong capitalization and ample liquidity serving as formidable defenses. This financial soundness is further reinforced by the Central Bank of the UAE's (CBUAE) vigilant watch, its proactive approach to monitoring and mitigating financial stability risks ensuring that any potential threats are swiftly identified and neutralized. The report also notes the banking sector's impressive profitability, a testament to its strength, driven by higher interest income resulting from rising interest rates and the steady influx of private credit, a sign of continued confidence in the UAE's economic prowess.

However, even the most formidable fortress has its vulnerabilities. The report acknowledges the persistence of certain exposures within the financial system, particularly to the real estate sector, a potential chink in the armor. To further enhance the robustness of the UAE's financial citadel and amplify its allure to investors seeking a safe and prosperous harbor, the IMF report recommends several key fortifications:

1. **Strengthening Macroprudential Frameworks: Reinforcing the Financial Ramparts**

A strategic plan is vital to further reinforce the UAE's financial ramparts, ensuring stability and resilience in the face of evolving challenges:

Effective Supervision of Digital Innovation and Fintech Activities: Guiding the Fintech Surge: The rapid ascent of digital innovation and fintech presents both golden opportunities and potential pitfalls for the financial sector, akin to navigating uncharted waters filled with both promise and peril. The UAE must ensure effective supervision of these activities to mitigate potential risks while nurturing the spirit of innovation. This requires a deft hand at the helm, steering a course that embraces progress while safeguarding stability. Key maneuvers include:

Developing robust regulatory frameworks for fintech companies, addressing issues such as data privacy, cybersecurity, and consumer protection: Establishing clear rules of engagement for fintech companies is crucial, safeguarding the interests of consumers and businesses alike as they navigate this uncharted territory.

Enhancing the CBUAE's supervisory capacity to effectively monitor and regulate fintech activities: Empowering the CBUAE with the tools and expertise to effectively oversee the rapidly evolving fintech landscape is essential to ensure responsible innovation and mitigate potential risks.

Promoting responsible innovation in the financial sector, encouraging the development of fintech solutions that benefit consumers and businesses while maintaining financial stability: Fostering a culture of responsible innovation within the financial sector ensures that technological advancements serve the greater good, propelling economic growth while preserving financial stability.

Continued Monitoring of Financial Stability Risks: Maintaining a Watchful Eye: Maintaining a vigilant watch on the horizon is recommended, constantly monitoring financial stability risks, particularly in light of evolving challenges:

High Level of Nonperforming Loans (NPLs): Navigating Troubled Waters: While NPLs have receded from their pandemic peak, they remain elevated compared to historical levels, like a receding tide revealing hidden shoals. The CBUAE should continue to monitor NPL trends, encouraging banks to chart a course toward reducing these troubled loans and ensuring adequate provisioning to weather any potential storms.

Tightening Financial Conditions: Adjusting to Shifting Winds: Rising interest rates and global economic uncertainty can create headwinds for borrowers, potentially leading to increased NPLs and financial stress. The CBUAE should closely monitor these developments and implement appropriate macroprudential measures, like adjusting the sails to changing winds, to mitigate risks and ensure a smooth voyage for the UAE's financial system.

Banks' Exposures to Real Estate: Navigating the Property Seas: The real estate sector remains a potential area of vulnerability, a sea that can be both calm and turbulent. The CBUAE should maintain a watchful eye on banks' exposures to real estate, ensuring strict adherence to existing prudential regulations and considering additional safeguards, like reinforcing the hull of the financial ship, to mitigate potential risks.

2. **Strengthening the AML/CFT Framework: Guarding Against Illicit Tides**

The UAE's progress in bolstering its Anti-Money Laundering and Combating the Financing of Terrorism (AML/CFT) framework under the National AML/CFT Strategy and Action Plan is noticeable, recognizing the nation's commitment to safeguarding the integrity of its financial system. However, the report urges continued vigilance, urging the UAE to further strengthen its defences against illicit financial flows:

Addressing Remaining Deficiencies: Sealing the Cracks: The significant progress made is welcomed but emphasizes the need to address remaining vulnerabilities identified by the Financial Action Task Force (FATF), like sealing any cracks in the fortress walls that could be exploited by illicit actors. This includes:

- **Enhancing beneficial ownership transparency to prevent the misuse of corporate structures for illicit activities**: Shining a light on the true owners of corporate entities helps prevent their misuse for nefarious purposes, ensuring that the UAE's financial system remains a beacon of transparency and integrity.

- **Strengthening the CBUAE's supervisory capacity to effectively monitor and enforce AML/CFT regulations**: Empowering the CBUAE with the resources and expertise to effectively enforce AML/CFT regulations is essential to deterring financial crime and safeguarding the UAE's reputation as a trusted financial hub.

- **Enhancing international cooperation in AML/CFT matters to combat cross-border financial crimes**: Collaboration with international partners is crucial to combating financial crime, as criminals often operate across borders, requiring a united front to effectively counter their illicit activities.

Additional Recommendations: Polishing the Jewels of the Financial Crown

The following presents a collection of additional blueprints, designed to further enhance the brilliance of the UAE's financial crown:

Promoting Effective Management of Legacy NPLs: Transforming Challenges into Triumphs: The CBUAE should encourage banks to adopt a proactive approach to managing and reducing legacy NPLs, like skilled artisans meticulously restoring a masterpiece to its former glory. This could involve strategic loan restructuring, well-timed asset sales, or, when necessary, decisive write-offs, all while ensuring adequate provisioning to safeguard against future storms.

Further Strengthening Regulation and Supervision of the Insurance Sector: Shielding Against Uncertainty: The insurance sector stands as a critical pillar of financial stability, providing a safety net against life's unexpected turns. The UAE should continue to fortify the walls surrounding this vital sector, strengthening its regulation and supervision to ensure its soundness, resilience, and ability to weather any storm.

Carefully Balancing Opportunities and Risks Associated with

Digital Innovation: Navigating the Digital Frontier with Prudence: While embracing the boundless potential of digital innovation, the UAE must also navigate the digital frontier with prudence, carefully assessing and mitigating potential risks associated with new technologies and business models in the banking and payments sector. This includes prioritizing cybersecurity, safeguarding data privacy, and ensuring robust consumer protection, creating a secure and trustworthy environment for innovation to flourish.

By meticulously implementing these recommendations, the UAE can further enhance the splendor and allure of its financial crown, attracting even greater investment, nurturing a culture of groundbreaking innovation, and solidifying its position as a leading global financial center, a shining beacon in the world of finance. This proactive approach to strengthening the financial sector not only fuels the UAE's economic engine, propelling growth and stability, but also burnishes its reputation as a safe, secure, and reliable haven for discerning international investors and businesses seeking a prosperous and trustworthy partner.

Opportunities Amidst Transformation: Unveiling the UAE's Tapestry of Potential

The UAE is undergoing a breathtaking metamorphosis, its economic landscape transforming into a vibrant tapestry of opportunity woven with threads of diversification, innovation, and sustainability. The IMF report illuminates several key areas ripe for investment, inviting businesses and investors to explore the UAE's dynamic growth trajectory and unearth the treasures that await:

1. **Digitalization: The Spark Igniting Growth and Diversification**

The UAE is investing heavily in constructing a robust digital infrastructure, laying the groundwork for a future empowered by cutting-edge technologies. This digital renaissance is creating fertile ground for businesses operating in the digital sphere, a landscape teeming with opportunity waiting to be cultivated. This digital transformation is unlocking a treasure chest of possibilities across various sectors:

E-commerce: A Blossoming Marketplace: The UAE's e-commerce market is experiencing explosive growth, fueled by widespread internet and smartphone penetration, a young and tech-savvy population eager to embrace new possibilities, and a burgeoning preference for the convenience and accessibility of online shopping. This digital marketplace presents a golden opportunity for innovative e-commerce platforms, forward-thinking online retailers, and agile logistics providers equipped to navigate this dynamic landscape.

Fintech: A Hub of Financial Innovation: The UAE is rapidly transforming into a regional fintech powerhouse, a magnet for both groundbreaking startups and established financial institutions seeking to ride the wave of digital disruption. The government's supportive regulatory environment, coupled with a burgeoning demand for convenient and accessible digital financial services, is fueling rapid growth in areas such as mobile payments, digital banking, and blockchain technology, creating fertile ground for innovation to flourish.

Artificial Intelligence (AI): Unlocking the Power of Intelligent Machines: The UAE is positioning itself as a global pioneer in the realm of artificial intelligence, making strategic investments in research and development, attracting top talent from around the globe, and nurturing the development of AI-powered solutions across a wide array of sectors. This dedication to harnessing the power of intelligent machines is already transforming industries such as healthcare, education, transportation, and government services, paving the way for a more efficient, responsive, and innovative future.

The transformative potential of AI and digitalization is recognizable, urging continued investment in enabling infrastructure to further diversify the UAE's economic landscape and pave a smooth path toward a sustainable and energy-efficient future..

2.   Green Initiatives: Cultivating a Sustainable Oasis

The UAE is demonstrating an unwavering commitment to environmental stewardship, not only envisioning a greener future but actively cultivating it. The nation has set ambitious targets to achieve net-zero emissions by 2050, a testament to its dedication to creating a sustainable oasis amidst the desert landscape. This commitment is blossoming into a flourishing garden of opportunities in the green sector:

Renewable Energy: Harnessing the Power of the Sun: The UAE is basking in the glow of its solar energy investments, funneling substantial resources into harnessing the abundant power of the sun. The country proudly boasts some of the world's largest and most cost-effective solar projects, transforming its landscape into a shimmering sea of solar panels, solidifying its position as a global leader in the transition toward clean and sustainable energy.

Green Finance: Nurturing Sustainable Growth: The UAE is cultivating a fertile ecosystem for green finance, nurturing the growth of sustainable investments and pioneering innovative financing mechanisms for environmentally friendly projects. This includes the issuance of green bonds, establishing specialized green banks, and carefully crafting sustainable finance regulations, ensuring that financial flows are directed toward a greener and more sustainable future.

Sustainable Infrastructure: Building a Foundation for a Brighter Future: The UAE is prioritizing the development of sustainable infrastructure, embedding green building standards, energy-efficient designs, and eco-friendly materials into the very fabric of its construction projects. This unwavering focus on sustainability is creating fertile ground for companies specializing in green building technologies, sustainable construction materials, and energy-efficient solutions to thrive, as the nation constructs a future that harmonizes with the environment.

It is of a critical importance to adopt a balanced approach to energy transition, advocating for a scaling up of investments in renewable and clean energy sources while simultaneously encouraging the "greening" of existing extraction processes in the hydrocarbon sector. This harmonious approach aims to ensure energy security while minimizing environmental impact and fostering a path toward lasting sustainable development.

3. Trade and Tourism: Expanding the UAE's Global Embrace

The UAE is strategically extending its global embrace, forging new trade partnerships and crafting world-class tourism experiences that captivate visitors from around the globe. These efforts are unlocking a treasure trove of opportunities for businesses operating in these dynamic sectors:

Trade: Building Bridges of Prosperity: The UAE is actively pursuing Comprehensive Economic Partnership Agreements (CEPAs) with key trading partners worldwide, carefully constructing bridges of economic cooperation and shared prosperity. These agreements aim to dismantle barriers to trade, boost the flow of exports, and attract foreign investment, further diversifying the nation's economic tapestry and weaving the UAE into the intricate fabric of global value chains. The UAE's progress on CEPAs, recognizing their potential to stimulate trade, attract foreign direct investment, and strengthen the UAE's integration into the global marketplace.

Tourism: Crafting Unforgettable Experiences: The UAE has become synonymous with world-class tourism, its iconic destinations attracting millions of eager visitors each year. The nation continuously invests in crafting new and unforgettable experiences, expanding and enhancing its hospitality infrastructure, and offering a kaleidoscope of diverse tourism offerings. This unwavering dedication to creating a world-class tourism destination creates a playground of opportunity for businesses in the hospitality, travel, and leisure sectors, as the UAE continues to enchant visitors from around the globe.

The UAE's strategic focus on strengthening existing trade partnerships while forging new ones, coupled with its dedication to curating exceptional tourism experiences, further solidifies its position as a global hub for both business and leisure, a crossroads where cultures converge and opportunities abound. These efforts attract investment, generate employment opportunities, and infuse the nation's economy with vibrancy and growth.

The UAE's economic transformation is unfolding like an intricate and beautiful tapestry, a testament to the nation's ambition, vision, and unwavering commitment to progress. This evolving landscape presents a compelling array of opportunities for discerning investors and businesses seeking to weave their own success stories into the fabric of the UAE's future. By capitalizing on these opportunities, particularly in the thriving arenas of digitalization, green initiatives, and the interconnected worlds of trade and tourism, investors can not only contribute to the UAE's continued economic success but also reap the rewards of participating in this dynamic and burgeoning market. The UAE's message to the world is clear: the time to invest is now, as this extraordinary nation continues its journey toward an even brighter and more prosperous tomorrow.

Key Takeaways for Investors: Navigating the UAE's Ever-Shifting Sands

The UAE's economic landscape, like the desert that surrounds it, is a dynamic and ever-shifting terrain, ripe with opportunity for those who know how to navigate its contours. While the potential rewards are abundant, success requires a strategic compass, a long-term vision, and a keen understanding of both the shimmering mirages and the hidden oases that dot this landscape.

1. **Strategic Partnerships: Unlocking the Secrets of the Desert**

Venturing into the UAE's business landscape without forging alliances with local partners is akin to navigating the desert without a seasoned guide. Local partners offer invaluable wisdom and resources, helping investors navigate the intricate paths to success:

Regulatory Expertise: Deciphering the Ancient Scrolls: Navigating the labyrinthine pathways of the UAE's regulatory landscape can be daunting for outsiders. Local partners, well-versed in the ancient scrolls of local laws, regulations, and time-honored business practices, act as trusted advisors, guiding investors away from potential pitfalls and ensuring seamless compliance with the land's rules.

Market Insights: Unveiling Hidden Oases: Local partners possess an intimate understanding of the UAE's economic ecosystem, like desert nomads who can read the subtle signs of the sand dunes. They provide crucial insights into market dynamics, consumer preferences, and the competitive landscape, empowering investors to make informed decisions and tailor their strategies to discover the hidden oases of opportunity.

Network Access: Unlocking the Gates to Influence: Local partners have spent years cultivating a web of connections, their networks extending like ancient trade routes to key stakeholders, including influential government officials, respected business leaders, and potential customers. This access to the corridors of power and influence can unlock doors and facilitate invaluable introductions, paving the way for fruitful collaborations and accelerating the path to success.

Cultural Understanding: Speaking the Language of Trust: Understanding the UAE's rich cultural tapestry and unspoken rules of engagement is as crucial as navigating by the stars. Local partners act as cultural interpreters, bridging cultural divides, ensuring smooth and respectful communication, and fostering trust, the most valuable currency in this land of opportunity.

2. **Long-Term Vision: Aligning with the Stars of the UAE's 2050 Strategies**

Investors seeking enduring success in the UAE must adopt a long-term perspective, aligning their ambitions with the guiding stars of the UAE's 2050 strategies, a roadmap to a brighter and more prosperous future:

Economic Diversification: Seeding a Multifaceted Oasis: The UAE is actively reducing its reliance on oil, its economy blossoming like a vibrant oasis with diverse sources of growth. Investments in sectors like tourism, logistics, manufacturing, technology, and renewable energy, aligned with this diversification strategy, are like seeds sown in fertile ground, poised to flourish with government support and benefit from the nation's long-term growth trajectory.

Private Sector Growth: Fueling the Engine of Prosperity: The UAE recognizes that the private sector is the lifeblood of its economy, the engine that drives innovation and prosperity for all. Projects that nourish the private sector, creating employment opportunities and fostering a spirit of entrepreneurship, are like precious water poured onto the desert sands, fuelling growth and ensuring a vibrant and sustainable future.

Sustainability: Cultivating a Legacy for Generations: The UAE is deeply committed to preserving its environment for future generations, investing in green technologies, harnessing the power of renewable energy, and constructing sustainable infrastructure. Projects aligned with this vision of sustainability, contributing to the UAE's net-zero emissions target, are like precious date palms planted in the desert, offering shade, sustenance, and a legacy of responsible stewardship for generations to come.

3. Due Diligence: Reading the Shifting Sands of Risk and Opportunity

While the UAE's economic landscape shimmers with promise, wise investors know that thorough due diligence is paramount to avoid mirages and navigate the terrain with a keen eye and a steady hand:

Weaker Global Growth: Weathering the Global Sandstorms: Global economic headwinds, like sandstorms blowing across the desert, can impact the UAE's growth trajectory, particularly in sectors such as tourism, trade, and investment. Savvy investors must carefully assess the potential impact of these global forces on their projects and develop contingency plans, like seeking shelter in an oasis, to weather any storm.

Tighter Financial Conditions: Navigating Shifting Sands: Rising interest rates and global financial market volatility can create challenges akin to shifting sand dunes, potentially increasing borrowing costs and restricting access to capital. Investors must carefully evaluate their financing options and ensure they have sufficient capital reserves, like a camel carrying precious water, to navigate these shifting sands and emerge stronger.

Geopolitical Developments: Reading the Winds of Change: Regional and global geopolitical tensions, like unpredictable desert winds, can stir up uncertainty and impact investor sentiment. Wise investors must closely monitor these geopolitical developments, interpreting the subtle shifts in the wind to assess their potential implications for their investments and adjust their course accordingly.

Energy Transition: Embracing the Winds of Change: The global shift toward a lower-carbon economy presents both challenges and remarkable opportunities for the UAE, like a changing desert landscape revealing hidden springs of innovation. Investors must carefully assess the potential impact of this energy transition on their projects, considering both the risks associated with declining oil demand and the exciting opportunities presented by the burgeoning renewable energy sector.

The UAE extends a welcoming hand to investors, but successfully navigating its dynamic landscape requires more than just a spirit of adventure. It demands a strategic compass, a trusted guide, and a willingness to embrace both the challenges and the rewards that await. By forging strategic partnerships with those who know the terrain, aligning their aspirations with the UAE's long-term vision, and employing meticulous due diligence, investors can confidently navigate the shifting sands of risk and opportunity, ultimately contributing to the UAE's continued economic success while reaping the rewards of their well-placed trust.

Chapter Conclusion: The UAE's Financial System - A Beacon of Stability and Opportunity in a Turbulent World

This chapter has journeyed through the UAE's dynamic economic landscape, drawing wisdom from the IMF's June 2023 Article IV Consultation report, a treasure map guiding us through this land of opportunity. The UAE's ongoing transformation, fueled by its bold diversification strategy and unwavering commitment to sustainable growth, paints a compelling saga of resilience, innovation, and boundless potential.

The nation's remarkable ability to not only navigate the turbulent waters of the post-pandemic recovery but to emerge stronger, attracting safe-haven inflows and orchestrating major IPOs even as global uncertainty casts its shadow, is a testament to its robust economic foundations and the unwavering confidence it inspires in investors worldwide. The UAE's proactive approach to fiscal management, characterized by prudent stewardship of its resources, strategic efforts to broaden its revenue base, and a commitment to optimizing expenditure efficiency, further strengthens its economic bulwarks.

The UAE's financial system, a beacon of stability and resilience, continues to evolve and adapt, embracing the transformative power of digital innovation while diligently addressing vulnerabilities, particularly those related to the ever-evolving real estate sector. The ongoing reinforcement of its macroprudential frameworks and the unwavering dedication to strengthening its AML/CFT regime further enhance the UAE's allure as a global financial hub, a magnet for investors seeking a secure and prosperous harbor for their capital.

The Arabian Gulf Economic & Investment Ecosystem

The UAE's journey of economic transformation has unveiled a treasure trove of opportunities for investors, particularly in the burgeoning fields of digitalization, green initiatives, and the interconnected worlds of trade and tourism. However, navigating this dynamic landscape requires more than just a thirst for adventure; it demands a strategic compass and a willingness to embrace a long-term perspective. Investors must forge strong partnerships with local entities, tapping into their invaluable expertise, align their aspirations with the guiding stars of the UAE's 2050 strategies, and employ meticulous due diligence to navigate the shifting sands of risk and opportunity, particularly those arising from global economic tides and the ongoing energy transition.

The UAE, with its unwavering commitment to diversification, innovation, and building a sustainable future, stands tall as a beacon of economic progress in a world grappling with uncertainty. By embracing a strategic and informed approach, investors can not only contribute to the UAE's continued success story but also reap the rewards of participating in this dynamic and ever-evolving market, a testament to human ingenuity and the power of collaboration.

CHAPTER 5

Kuwait: Charting a New Course Amidst a Sea of Riches

Kuwait, a nation shimmering with the riches of black gold, stands at a pivotal crossroads. While soaring oil prices have propelled a remarkable recovery, painting a rosy picture of fiscal and external balances, the nation must now confront the deeply ingrained structural challenges that lie beneath the surface. This chapter, drawing wisdom from different sources including the International Monetary Fund's (IMF) September 2023 Article IV Consultation report, embarks on a journey through Kuwait's economic landscape, illuminating both the glittering peaks of its success and the shadowed valleys where reform is urgently needed.

Beyond the Gusher: A Tale of Tenacity and Transformation

Kuwait's story is inextricably woven with the threads of oil, a resource that has indelibly shaped its destiny. While this liquid gold has fueled breathtaking wealth and economic expansion, it has also cultivated a dependence that casts a long shadow on the nation's future prosperity.

Non-Oil Sector: A Phoenix Rising, Yet Winds of Change Blow

The non-oil sector, like a phoenix, has demonstrated remarkable resilience in recent years, emerging from the ashes of the pandemic-induced contraction. Growth soared to an estimated 3.4 percent in 2021, propelled by the resurgence of domestic and external demand. This momentum surged onward in 2022, with non-oil GDP growth accelerating to a robust 4.0 percent, fueled by the continued recovery in external demand and a diminishing fiscal drag. This tenacious spirit is a testament to the inherent strength of the Kuwaiti economy and the government's unwavering commitment to nurturing its non-oil sectors.

However, the IMF report sounds a cautionary note, emphasizing that this growth alone is not sufficient to quench the thirst of a rapidly burgeoning and youthful population. With a wave of approximately 100,000 young Kuwaitis poised to enter the workforce within the next five years, the non-oil sector must transform into a dynamic engine of job creation. This demographic tide, coupled with the global currents shifting towards decarbonization and the inevitable ebb of oil revenues, elevates economic diversification from a mere ambition to an urgent imperative for Kuwait.

The Symphony of Diversification: An Urgent Overture

There is a critical need for Kuwait to orchestrate a swift and expansive diversification of its economy. This signifies a departure from the familiar rhythm of oil dependence and the creation of a vibrant, multifaceted private sector, a symphony of innovation capable of generating high-quality jobs and conducting sustainable growth. Several compelling themes underscore the urgency of this transformation:

Diminishing Oil Revenues: The global overture towards renewable energy sources and the gradual diminuendo of oil demand will inevitably impact Kuwait's oil revenues, making it crucial to compose alternative sources of income.

Job Creation for a Young Orchestra: The arrival of a new generation of Kuwaitis into the workforce necessitates the composition of a vast repertoire of new jobs, a demand that the public sector alone cannot meet.

Enhancing Competitiveness: Kuwait's competitiveness has experienced a subtle dissonance in recent years, partly due to the high notes of labor costs and the softer melodies of productivity. Diversification into sectors with greater value-added potential can help harmonize Kuwait's economic tune, attracting foreign investment and orchestrating a brighter future.

Unlocking Kuwait's Potential: A Crescendo of Opportunity

Despite the challenges, Kuwait possesses an arsenal of strengths, instruments capable of composing a masterpiece of economic diversification. These include:

Abundant Financial Resources: Kuwait's sovereign wealth fund, a treasure chest overflowing with assets, provides a powerful instrument, a financial baton capable of strategically conducting diversification efforts.

A Well-Educated Population: Kuwait boasts a highly educated populace, a chorus of minds eager to learn and contribute, representing a potent force in the composition of a knowledge-based economy.

Strategic Location: Kuwait's strategic location, nestled in the heart of the Gulf region, provides a coveted stage, offering access to a vast and ever-expanding market.

By addressing the structural bottlenecks, investing in the virtuosity of its human capital, and fostering a more dynamic and competitive private sector, Kuwait can conduct a symphony of economic diversification, creating a harmonious and sustainable melody that will resonate for generations to come.

Riding the Fiscal Wave: Balancing Today's Bounty with Tomorrow's Horizon

Kuwait's fiscal landscape has undergone a dramatic transformation, sailing from the turbulent seas of deficits to the calm waters of substantial surpluses. This remarkable turnaround is largely attributed to the windfall of surging oil revenues, coupled with a degree of restraint in navigating expenditure currents. The overall fiscal balance, like a buoy lifted by the tide, has risen to a surplus of 6.5 percent of GDP in FY2021/22. The IMF report predicts even sunnier skies, forecasting a surge to 23.4 percent of GDP in FY2022/23. However, beneath this glittering surface of fiscal prosperity lie submerged reefs that demand careful navigation to ensure a sustainable voyage for generations to come.

The Siren Song of Surplus: Heeding the Call for Fiscal Prudence

While the current fiscal surpluses might sing a siren song of abundance, a cautionary view against succumbing to complacency is required. The heavy reliance on the capricious nature of oil revenues leaves Kuwait's fiscal ship vulnerable to sudden storms in the global oil market. Furthermore, the current spending structure, resembling a grand but inefficient vessel with its large public sector wage bill and generous energy subsidies, is not built for a long and sustainable journey.

Charting a Course to Safe Harbor: Guiding Stars

The fiscal consolidation is of critical importance, urging Kuwait to set its compass towards long-term sustainability and intergenerational equity. This means taking advantage of the current fair winds to build fiscal buffers, sturdy reserves to weather future economic squalls and ensure that today's spending does not leave future generations stranded on the shores of debt.

It is recommended to have a growth-friendly fiscal consolidation scenario, a course that balances the need for prudent navigation with the objective of reaching the destination of robust economic growth and diversification. This course encompasses both revenue and expenditure adjustments, with the following key points on the map:

Revenue Enhancement: Discovering New Treasures:

Implementing a GCC-wide VAT and Excises: Introducing a VAT and excises on tobacco and sugary drinks, in harmony with agreements among GCC countries, would provide a steady stream of non-oil revenue, like discovering a hidden spring on a seemingly barren island.

Expanding Corporate Income Taxation: Casting the net wider to encompass domestic companies within the corporate income tax base would enhance revenue collection, ensuring all vessels contribute their fair share to the journey.

Enhancing Revenue Administration Capacity: Equipping the Ministry of Finance with the tools and expertise to navigate the complex waters of tax collection and revenue management is crucial to maximizing the bounty of existing revenue streams.

Expenditure Rationalization: Streamlining the Ship:

Curtailing the Wage Bill: Moderating public sector wage growth and aligning it with the prevailing currents in the private sector would lighten the fiscal load and encourage private sector employment, allowing the ship to move more swiftly.

Gradually Phasing Out Untargeted Energy Subsidies: Phasing out untargeted energy subsidies, while extending lifelines of support to vulnerable households, would reduce fiscal burdens, promote the efficient use of resources, and free up funds for investment in more productive endeavors, like charting new trade routes.

Improving the Efficiency of Capital Spending: Enhancing the planning, selection, and execution of capital projects, much like a skilled navigator charting the most efficient course, would ensure that investments are directed towards projects that promise the highest returns.

By implementing these recommendations, Kuwait can confidently navigate the fiscal currents, transforming potential hazards into opportunities for growth and ensuring a prosperous voyage towards a future where economic stability and diversification reign supreme..

Beyond Fiscal Shores: Charting a New Course with Structural Reforms

Simply navigating the fiscal seas, while crucial, will not be sufficient to reach the shores of a prosperous future. To truly unlock the treasure chest of private sector-led growth and achieve sustainable economic diversification, Kuwait must embark on a journey of deep-rooted structural reforms. These reforms are the compass and sextant needed to navigate the uncharted waters ahead.

Breaking Down Walls: Dismantling Labor Market Segmentation

Bridging the Wage Divide: The chasm between national and expatriate wages must be bridged to entice Kuwaitis to seek opportunities within the private sector, fostering a more inclusive and dynamic workforce.

Embracing Flexibility: Introducing greater agility into the hiring and firing processes would transform the labor market into a more responsive and efficient vessel, better equipped to weather economic storms and seize new opportunities.

Raising the Mast of Competitiveness

Investing in Human Capital: Like a ship investing in a skilled crew, Kuwait must prioritize education, training, and innovation to elevate productivity and steer its economy towards greater competitiveness on the global stage.

Leveling the Playing Field: Creating a business environment where fair competition reigns supreme and bureaucratic obstacles are minimized will attract ambitious entrepreneurs and allow the private sector to flourish.

Removing the Bottlenecks: Smoothing the Path for Business

Modernizing Land Allocation: Introducing transparent, market-based mechanisms for land allocation, akin to establishing clear navigation channels, will streamline investment and unlock the potential of this valuable resource.

Opening Doors to Foreign Investment: Relaxing restrictions on foreign ownership in strategic sectors will attract international capital and expertise, fostering healthy competition and propelling economic growth.

By embracing these structural reforms, Kuwait can transform its economic ship into a sleek and agile vessel, capable of navigating the complexities of the global economy and charting a course towards a brighter and more prosperous future.

A Tapestry of Transformation: Weaving a New Economic Narrative for Kuwait

Kuwait's future prosperity lies not in clinging to the familiar shores of oil dependence, but in setting sail towards a vibrant new horizon, one where a dynamic and competitive private sector powers economic growth. Achieving this vision requires weaving a comprehensive tapestry of reforms, addressing the deeply ingrained structural knots that bind the nation's economic potential. A blueprint for this transformation, highlighting four key threads:

1. **Labor Market Reforms: Unlocking the Potential of Human Capital**

Kuwait's labor market currently resembles a divided tapestry, with a stark separation between the public and private sectors. The public sector, with its alluring threads of high wages, generous benefits, and job security, has drawn a disproportionate number of Kuwaiti nationals, leaving the private sector yearning for skilled hands. This imbalance has created a series of knots:

- **Stifling Private Sector Growth**: The dominance of the public sector casts a long shadow on private enterprise, limiting opportunities for expansion and job creation.
- **Wage Disparities and Misaligned Skills**: The chasm between national and expatriate wages discourages Kuwaitis from seeking opportunities within the private sector, leading to a misallocation of talent and hindering economic progress.
- **Productivity Slump**: The lack of competition and performance-based incentives within the public sector has resulted in a slackening of productivity, slowing the momentum of economic growth.

To untangle these knots, the IMF proposes a series of bold strokes:

- **Harmonizing Wage Structures**: Gradually aligning public sector wages with those in the private sector would bridge the wage gap, encouraging Kuwaitis to contribute their skills to the burgeoning private sector.

- **Embracing Labor Market Flexibility**: Introducing greater fluidity in hiring and firing practices would transform the labor market into a more responsive and efficient loom, allowing businesses to adapt to changing market demands and weave new patterns of success.

- **Streamlining Expatriate Labor Policies**: Relaxing restrictions on expatriate labor, such as visa requirements and sponsorship regulations, would attract skilled artisans from abroad, enriching the tapestry of Kuwait's workforce and enhancing the competitiveness of the private sector.

2. Social Safety Net Enhancement: Providing a Safety Net for Transformation

Labor market reforms, while essential, can temporarily disrupt the existing order, potentially leading to job displacement and income loss for some workers. To ensure that no one is left behind in this transformation, there is a clear need to strengthen the social safety net via:

- **Enhancing Efficiency and Targeting**: Refining the targeting and efficiency of social assistance programs, such as unemployment benefits and job training initiatives, would provide a crucial lifeline for workers navigating the transition, ensuring they have the support to land on their feet.

- **Investing in Skills Development**: Expanding vocational training programs and creating pathways for skills upgrading would equip workers with the tools and knowledge needed to thrive in a diversified economy, empowering them to contribute to new sectors and industries.

- **Promoting Active Labor Market Policies**: Strengthening job search assistance and offering incentives for private sector employment would act as guiding threads, helping displaced workers reintegrate into the workforce and find fulfilling roles in the evolving economy.

3. Business Environment Improvements: Cultivating Fertile Ground for Investment

Kuwait's business environment, while possessing potential, faces a series of obstacles that resemble a tangled thicket, hindering the growth of the private sector. Bureaucratic hurdles, restrictions on foreign ownership, and a lack of competition in key sectors create a challenging landscape for businesses to thrive. To clear these obstacles and plant the seeds for a more fertile business environment, it is recommended to:

- **Streamline Business Procedures**: Like pruning away dead branches, simplifying and digitizing business registration, licensing, and permitting processes would reduce administrative burdens, allowing entrepreneurs to focus on innovation and growth.

- **Welcome Foreign Investment**: Easing restrictions on foreign ownership in select sectors would attract international capital and expertise, like fresh rain nourishing thirsty ground, fostering healthy competition and cross-pollination of ideas.

- **Optimize Land Allocation**: Implementing transparent, market-based mechanisms for land allocation, akin to carefully tilling the soil, would ensure this valuable resource is directed towards its most productive uses, yielding the greatest economic harvest.

- **Nurturing Competition**: Strengthening the enforcement of competition laws and ensuring a level playing field for all businesses, like removing weeds that stifle growth, would encourage innovation, efficiency, and a vibrant marketplace.

4. Investment in Human Capital: Sowing the Seeds of a Knowledge-Based Economy

Kuwait possesses a valuable asset in its well-educated population, yet there remains untapped potential in nurturing the quality of education and aligning skills with the needs of the private sector. The IMF report stresses the importance of cultivating this human capital to harvest the fruits of a knowledge-based economy:

- **Enhancing Education Quality**: Like enriching the soil with vital nutrients, improving the quality of education at all levels, from primary to tertiary, is crucial to developing a skilled and adaptable workforce, ready to meet the challenges of a changing world.

- **Expanding Vocational Training**: Providing wider access to vocational training programs, like offering specialized tools for specific tasks, would equip students with practical skills that directly translate to the needs of the private sector, ensuring a pipeline of talent ready to contribute.

- **Fostering Research and Innovation**: Investing in research and development and nurturing collaboration between universities and businesses, much like grafting new ideas onto existing knowledge, would stimulate innovation and create a fertile ecosystem for a more knowledge-intensive economy to blossom.

A long-term vision for sustainable prosperity is the guiding principle for Kuwait's economic journey. Implementing this comprehensive package of reforms requires a sustained and coordinated effort, a shared commitment to tending the fields of progress from the government, the private sector, and civil society. It demands a steadfast focus on long-term growth and shared prosperity over quick gains. By embracing this transformative agenda, Kuwait can cultivate a future where its full economic potential is realized, and its citizens reap a bountiful harvest of opportunity and prosperity.

Unveiling Kuwait's Investment Jewels: A Treasure Map for the Savvy Investor

Discerning investors can leverage these insights to unearth promising prospects and contribute to Kuwait's metamorphosis into a diversified and thriving economy. Here are some of the glittering gems revealed:

Digitalization and Technology: Mining the Gold of the Digital Frontier

- **Fintech**: Kuwait's robust and well-capitalized banking sector, combined with a tech-savvy young population, presents fertile ground for fintech innovation. Opportunities abound in areas like mobile payments, digital banking, and online lending platforms, promising rich returns for those who stake their claim early.

- **E-commerce**: The pandemic ignited a surge in e-commerce adoption, creating a gold rush for online retailers, logistics providers, and digital payment solutions, all vying for a share of this rapidly expanding market.

- **Digital Infrastructure**: Investing in the underlying infrastructure of the digital economy, including high-speed internet, data centers, and cybersecurity, is akin to building the railroads of the digital age, essential for connecting businesses and consumers in this new frontier.

Renewable Energy and Sustainability: Cultivating a Greener Future

Solar Energy: Kuwait's abundant sunshine makes it a natural powerhouse for solar energy. Investments in solar power generation, solar panel manufacturing, and energy storage solutions are akin to planting seeds that will yield a sustainable and profitable harvest for years to come.

- **Green Buildings and Infrastructure**: As Kuwait seeks to reduce its environmental footprint, opportunities flourish in green building construction, energy-efficient infrastructure development, and sustainable transportation solutions, creating a legacy of responsible growth.

- **Waste Management and Recycling**: Investing in modern waste management and recycling facilities is not just environmentally responsible but also presents a lucrative opportunity to transform waste into valuable resources, fuelling a circular economy.

Tourism and Hospitality: Unlocking the Treasures of Arabian Hospitality

- **Luxury Tourism**: Kuwait possesses the allure to captivate high-end travellers with its blend of rich cultural heritage, modern infrastructure, and proximity to other Gulf destinations. Investments in luxury hotels, resorts, and unique tourism experiences promise to attract this discerning clientele.

- **Cultural and Heritage Tourism**: Kuwait's historical sites, museums, and cultural events offer a rich tapestry for investments in cultural and heritage tourism, breathing new life into restoration projects, visitor centers, and captivating cultural tours.

- **Business and MICE Tourism**: Kuwait's strategic position as a regional business hub can be further fortified through investments in state-of-the-art conference centers, exhibition facilities, and business hotels, attracting a steady stream of MICE (Meetings, Incentives, Conferences, and Exhibitions) tourism.

Education and Training: Shaping the Future Workforce

- **Private Education**: The demand for world-class education in Kuwait creates a wealth of opportunities for investments in private schools, universities, and specialized training institutions, shaping the leaders and innovators of tomorrow.

- **Vocational Training**: Expanding vocational training programs, tailoring them to the needs of a diversified economy, presents fertile ground for investments in technical schools, apprenticeship programs, and skills development centers, equipping the future workforce with in-demand skills.

- **Ed-Tech**: The surge in educational technology adoption opens doors for investments in edtech platforms, online learning solutions, and educational software, revolutionizing how knowledge is shared and acquired.

Healthcare: Investing in the Well-being of a Nation

- **Specialized Healthcare Services**: Kuwait's growing population and increasing demand for specialized healthcare services present a compelling opportunity for investments in state-of-the-art hospitals, clinics, and diagnostic centers, catering to a wide range of medical needs.

- Medical Tourism: By developing world-class healthcare facilities and offering competitive pricing, Kuwait can attract medical tourists seeking high-quality care, positioning itself as a regional leader in medical excellence.

- **Health-Tech**: Investments in health-tech solutions, such as telemedicine platforms, electronic health records, and healthcare data analytics, can revolutionize healthcare delivery, improving efficiency and expanding access for all.

By venturing into these promising investment territories, savvy investors can not only reap significant financial returns but also play a pivotal role in shaping a more dynamic, sustainable, and prosperous future for Kuwait.

Charting Your Course: A Mariner's Guide to the Kuwaiti Investment Seas

Kuwait's economic transformation is akin to a ship setting sail towards a new horizon, offering intrepid investors a unique opportunity to chart their own course towards growth and diversification. However, navigating these waters successfully requires a keen understanding of the currents and a strategic compass to steer towards long-term prosperity. Here's a mariner's guide to navigating the Kuwaiti investment seas:

1. **Navigating the Regulatory Environment: Charting a Safe Passage**

Deciphering the Charts: Kuwait's legal framework governing foreign investment, much like a detailed nautical chart, outlines the rules of engagement, covering company formation, foreign ownership, and repatriation of profits. Investors must meticulously study these charts to ensure compliance and avoid hidden shoals.

Securing Safe Harbor: Depending on the chosen course and cargo, investors may require various licenses and permits from different authorities, akin to obtaining clearances from different ports. This process demands careful planning and engagement with the relevant harbourmasters to ensure a smooth voyage.

Seeking Expert Navigation: Engaging seasoned legal and financial advisors specializing in Kuwaiti regulations is like having an experienced pilot on board, able to guide investors through intricate channels and ensure a safe and profitable passage.

2.   The Power of Local Partnerships: Sailing with a Seasoned Crew

Unlocking Local Knowledge: Local partners, much like seasoned sailors familiar with the local waters, possess invaluable insights into market dynamics, consumer preferences, and the competitive landscape, enabling investors to make informed decisions and avoid hidden reefs.

Navigating Cultural Currents: Understanding and respecting Kuwaiti culture and business practices is akin to mastering the art of navigating by the stars – essential for building strong relationships and fostering trust. Local partners can act as skilled navigators, guiding investors through cultural nuances and facilitating effective communication.

Leveraging Established Trade Routes: Local partners often boast well-established networks and connections with key stakeholders, like experienced merchants with access to exclusive trading routes. These connections can open doors for investors, providing access to government officials, business leaders, and potential customers.

3.   Embracing a Long-Term Vision: Setting a Course for Sustainable Success

Aligning with the North Star: Kuwait's Vision 2035, like the North Star guiding ancient mariners, outlines the country's long-term development aspirations, including economic diversification, human capital development, and sustainable growth. Investors who align their endeavors with this guiding star are more likely to receive favorable winds – government support – and contribute to the nation's collective voyage.

Patience and Persistence: Structural reforms and economic diversification, like long sea voyages, require time to bear fruit. Investors must demonstrate patience and persistence, weathering any storms along the way and recognizing that the full bounty of the Kuwaiti market may take time to materialize.

Building Seaworthy Vessels: Investors should focus on establishing sustainable businesses, crafting them like sturdy ships capable of weathering economic storms. These enterprises should create value for the Kuwaiti economy, generate employment opportunities, and contribute to the long-term prosperity of the nation.

4. Managing Risks and Challenges: Weathering the Inevitable Storms

Political Risks: Kuwait's political landscape, much like the open sea, can be unpredictable, with potential storms brewing that could impact investments. Staying informed about political developments and engaging with relevant stakeholders is akin to monitoring weather patterns, allowing investors to adjust their course and mitigate potential risks.

Economic Volatility: As an oil-exporting nation, Kuwait's economy can be susceptible to fluctuations in global oil prices, like a ship riding the waves of a volatile sea. Investors must factor in this inherent volatility and develop strategies to navigate potential economic downturns.

Competition: Kuwait's market is becoming increasingly competitive, with both local and international players vying for a share of the bounty, like ships competing for the best fishing grounds. Investors must develop a strong value proposition and a competitive edge to navigate these crowded waters and secure their share of the spoils.

5. Seizing the Opportunities: Discovering Uncharted Territories

First-Mover Advantage: Early investors in burgeoning sectors like renewable energy, technology, and tourism have the opportunity to become pioneers, the first to chart these uncharted territories and establish a dominant presence.

Government Incentives: The Kuwaiti government, like a benevolent ruler welcoming explorers, offers various incentives to attract foreign investment. These treasures include tax breaks, subsidies, and access to financing, all designed to reward those willing to invest in the nation's future.

Impact Investing: Investors seeking to make a positive social and environmental impact, charting a course towards a better future, will find ample opportunities in Kuwait's burgeoning focus on sustainability and social development.

In conclusion, Investing in Kuwait is not for the faint of heart; it demands a strategic compass, a discerning eye for opportunity, and the courage to navigate uncharted waters. By meticulously charting a course through the regulatory landscape, forging strong alliances with local partners, embracing a long-term vision like a steadfast captain, and skilfully manoeuvring around potential storms, investors can harness Kuwait's immense potential and ride the tide of its economic transformation.

Chapter Conclusion: A New Dawn Breaks on the Kuwaiti Horizon

Kuwait stands at a pivotal crossroads, a beacon shimmering between the familiar glow of its oil-fueled past and the radiant promise of a more diversified and sustainable future. While its abundant hydrocarbon wealth has provided a comfortable harbor, the winds of change are blowing, urging Kuwait to embrace a bold new course.

The need to navigate away from the shoals of complacency and set a course towards a transformative agenda is vital. The message is unmistakable: clinging to the old ways is no longer an option. Kuwait must confront its ingrained structural challenges, unleash the untapped potential of its people, and cultivate a dynamic private sector capable of weathering any storm and steering the nation toward a brighter future.

This voyage towards transformation demands a multi-faceted approach, a skilled crew working in unison:

- Fiscal Prudence: While current surpluses might create the illusion of calm seas, Kuwait must resist the siren song of complacency. Embracing fiscal consolidation is akin to battening down the hatches, building reserves for future storms and ensuring a legacy of prosperity for generations to come.
- Structural Reforms: Addressing labor market segmentation, raising the sails of competitiveness, and streamlining the business environment are akin to optimizing the ship's design, making it more agile, efficient, and capable of navigating the ever-changing currents of the global economy.
- Investment in Human Capital: Equipping Kuwait's workforce with the skills and knowledge needed for a diversified economy is like investing in a skilled and adaptable crew – the key to navigating uncharted waters and steering the ship towards success.

The journey ahead will be demanding, but Kuwait is a vessel built with the resilience of its people and the strength of its resources. Its vast financial reserves, a well-educated populace, and a strategic location provide a sturdy hull and a favorable wind. However, reaching the destination of lasting prosperity hinges on the determination to set a bold course, embrace innovation like a seasoned explorer, and foster a spirit of collaboration between the government, the private sector, and civil society – a united crew with a shared vision.

For investors, Kuwait represents a land of opportunity, an uncharted archipelago ripe for exploration. The nation's economic transformation is creating new channels for investment in sectors like technology, renewable energy, tourism, education, and healthcare – each a treasure island waiting to be discovered. However, navigating these promising waters requires more than just a map; it demands an understanding of the currents, a willingness to adapt, and the foresight to build lasting partnerships with those who know the local seas.

Kuwait's journey towards a diversified and sustainable economy is an epic tale waiting to be written. The ultimate success of this expedition rests on the choices made today by the government. By embracing the challenges as opportunities for growth and seizing the winds of change, Kuwait can chart a course toward a brighter future for its people, becoming a beacon of economic transformation in the region.

CHAPTER 6

Iraq: Unveiling the Investment Gems Beneath the Surface

Iraq: a land pulsating with untapped potential or shrouded in fiscal uncertainty? This chapter embarks on a journey through Iraq's evolving business landscape separating the glittering potential from the shadows of challenge. Discover how diversification efforts are taking root beyond the oil fields and uncover key insights for investors navigating this dynamic market.

Beyond the Headlines: Sensing the Pulse of Iraqi Investment

Iraq's allure as a potentially lucrative investment destination remains undeniable, but the narrative has taken on new dimensions. While significant opportunities beckon, like shimmering oases in the desert, a nuanced understanding of the current economic landscape is crucial for investors seeking to strike gold. This chapter delves into different sources including the insights gleaned from the International Monetary Fund's (IMF) April 2024 Article IV Consultation report, providing a compass to navigate both the challenges and the rewards of the Iraqi market.

Reconstruction and Rehabilitation: Unearthing a Multi-Billion Dollar Oasis

The commitment to rebuilding Iraq stands firm, a testament to the nation's resilience. The government's focus on fostering stability and social cohesion is noticeable, leading to significant investment in public services and infrastructure – fertile ground for international businesses to plant the seeds of growth, particularly in construction, engineering, and related sectors. The report highlights the government's prioritization of high-impact projects, like the Grand Al-Faw Port and the Karbala Refinery – beacons of opportunity for those seeking to make their mark on Iraq's resurgence. Let's excavate the details:

Scale of Investment: The IMF report projects that Iraq's capital expenditure will reach a significant 7% of GDP in 2024, a staggering figure representing trillions of Iraqi Dinars. This alone signals a gold rush for businesses specializing in infrastructure development.

Focus on Infrastructure: The report specifically underscores the government's commitment to "rehabilitating and recovering the educational system through additional infrastructures" and "upgrading critical infrastructure, including those related to information and communication technologies." This translates to a burgeoning demand for construction and engineering expertise in these vital sectors.

Electricity Sector Reform: The report emphasizes the urgent need to revitalize the electricity sector, currently grappling with inefficiency and unreliability. This presents a high-voltage opportunity for businesses specializing in power generation, transmission, and distribution, as well as those harnessing the power of renewable energy. The report suggests that "gradually moving towards cost recovery in the electricity sector could yield additional savings," a goal achievable through investments in domestic energy capacity and improvements in tariff collection.

Housing and Urban Development: With a population boom and rapid urbanization, the demand for housing and supporting infrastructure is soaring. There is a critical need for "significant and efficient investments" in various sectors, including housing, signalling a wealth of opportunities for businesses specializing in residential construction, urban planning, and development.

Transportation Networks: The report stresses the importance of "upgrading critical infrastructure," including the modernization of transportation networks. This paves the way for lucrative opportunities for businesses engaged in road construction, railway development, and airport expansion – building the arteries of Iraq's future growth.

The Iraqi government's unwavering dedication to reconstruction and rehabilitation, combined with the sheer scale of projected investment, transforms this sector into a multi-billion-dollar oasis for international businesses. By aligning their expertise with the government's priorities and leveraging their capabilities, businesses can play a pivotal role in rebuilding Iraq's infrastructure and contributing to its phoenix-like economic rise.

Beyond the Oil Fields: Cultivating a Multifaceted Economic Landscape

While oil continues to flow as a vital lifeblood for Iraq's economy, potentially gushing with US$5 trillion in revenues between 2013-2035, the nation is embarking on a journey of diversification, seeking new streams of prosperity. Structural reforms are imperative to unleash the dynamism of the private sector and cultivate growth in sectors beyond the oil fields. This fertile ground presents a wealth of opportunities for businesses ready to plant the seeds of innovation and reap the rewards of Iraq's transformation. Let's delve deeper into this burgeoning landscape:

Diversification: An Urgent Quest for Economic Resilience

Iraq's dependence on oil revenue is undeniable, exposing its vulnerability to the volatile tides of global oil prices. It cautions that "without additional diversification efforts, Iraq's external position is highly vulnerable to global energy transition risks." This serves as a clarion call for Iraq to nurture non-oil sectors, fostering a more robust and adaptable economy capable of weathering global storms.

Structural Reforms: Laying the Foundation for a Diverse Future

The report stresses that structural reforms are the bedrock upon which private sector-led growth and diversification can flourish. It offers a blueprint for action, recommending:

Labor Market Reforms: These include "leveling the playing field between public and private jobs," creating a more attractive environment for private sector employment; "strengthening institutional capacity to ensure an adequate work environment and labor protection," fostering a more productive and engaged workforce; and "addressing impediments to female labor participation," unlocking the potential of women in driving economic growth.

Business Environment Improvements: This entails "fixing the inefficient and unreliable electricity sector," providing a more stable and reliable power supply for businesses; "upgrading critical infrastructure," creating the backbone for efficient transportation, communication, and logistics; and "accelerating WTO accession," opening doors to global trade and investment.

Governance and Anti-Corruption Measures: The report emphasizes the need to fortify governance and combat corruption, fostering a transparent and accountable business environment. This includes strengthening public procurement frameworks, ensuring a fair and competitive marketplace, and streamlining business regulations to reduce bureaucracy and attract investment.

Sector-Specific Opportunities: Fields Ripe for Investment

Agriculture: Iraq boasts vast agricultural potential, but the sector faces challenges such as water scarcity, outdated farming practices, and limited access to finance. Investment in modern irrigation technologies, improved crop varieties, and enhanced agricultural infrastructure can unlock this sleeping giant, transforming it into a breadbasket of opportunity.

Manufacturing: Developing a diversified manufacturing base has the power to create jobs, reduce reliance on imports, and boost exports, solidifying Iraq's position in the global marketplace. Investment in light manufacturing, food processing, and building materials emerges as particularly promising, capitalizing on local resources and meeting growing domestic demand.

Services: The services sector, encompassing tourism, logistics, and financial services, holds immense potential to become a major engine of economic growth. Investing in infrastructure development, skills enhancement, and regulatory reforms can pave the way for these sectors to flourish, attracting investment and creating a more diversified and service-oriented economy.

Global Synergies: Harnessing the Power of International Partnerships

China's Belt and Road Initiative (BRI): The report recognizes the potential impact of the BRI on the region, including Iraq. The BRI's focus on infrastructure development, trade facilitation, and regional connectivity aligns seamlessly with Iraq's diversification goals, creating avenues for collaboration and growth. Businesses can leverage the BRI as a springboard to access funding, tap into Chinese expertise, and unlock new market opportunities.

Other International Partnerships: Iraq stands to benefit significantly from collaborations with other nations and international organizations eager to invest, transfer technology, and support the development of its non-oil sectors. These partnerships will be crucial in providing the expertise, resources, and market access needed to propel Iraq's diversification efforts forward.

Iraq's economic destiny hinges on its ability to successfully diversify, moving beyond its reliance on oil and harnessing the power of a multi-sector economy. By boldly implementing the recommended structural reforms, embracing innovation, and capitalizing on the potential of global partnerships, Iraq can cultivate a more resilient and diversified economy, one brimming with opportunities for businesses across a multitude of sectors..

Navigating the Fiscal Landscape: A Balancing Act on the Road to Reform

The IMF report provides a clear-eyed assessment of Iraq's fiscal landscape, acknowledging the rugged terrain while highlighting the government's determination to navigate it responsibly. While the report doesn't shy away from the challenges, it also recognizes the government's commitment to steering the economy towards a more sustainable path, a beacon of reassurance for those seeking to invest in Iraq's future. Let's examine the contours of this landscape in greater detail:

Challenges: Navigating the Headwinds

Widening Deficit: Iraq's fiscal deficit is projected to widen to 7.6% of GDP in 2024, a reflection of increased spending and the headwinds of declining oil prices. This widening gap underscores the need for decisive action to navigate towards a more balanced budget.

Rising Public Debt: the government debt could climb to over 86% of GDP by 2029 if the current course is maintained. This trajectory raises concerns about the long-term sustainability of debt levels and the potential for turbulence in the macroeconomic environment.

Large Public Wage Bill: The report identifies the weight of the public wage bill as a significant factor contributing to fiscal pressure. Mandatory hiring policies and generous public sector compensation have resulted in a public sector exceeding its ideal size, straining government coffers.

Declining Oil Prices: Factoring in the global energy landscape that assumes a decline in oil prices over the medium term will have significant impact on Iraq. This anticipated decline will further constrict government revenue, making the journey towards fiscal stability even more demanding.

Government's Responses: Steering Towards a Sustainable Course

Controlling Expenditure: The report acknowledges the government's efforts to rein in expenditure, particularly by addressing the elephant in the room – the public wage bill. This includes plans to phase out mandatory hiring policies and implement an attrition-based strategy to right-size public employment, making it more efficient and sustainable.

Mobilizing Non-Oil Revenues: Recognizing the need to diversify revenue streams, the government is actively pursuing strategies to boost non-oil revenue. This strategic shift involves:

Tax Policy Reforms: Implementing a payroll tax reform to create a fairer system, removing tax exemptions for profitable state-owned enterprises to level the playing field, and reviewing customs duties to optimize revenue collection.

Revenue Administration Improvements: Enhancing the use of the ASYCUDA system for more efficient customs management, implementing a self-assessment system for streamlined tax collection, and bolstering the capacity of the Large Taxpayer Office to ensure compliance among significant contributors.

Introducing New Taxes: Exploring the potential of introducing a general sales tax or VAT over the medium term, a strategic move to broaden the tax base and create a more stable revenue stream.

Strengthening Fiscal Management: The government is committed to enhancing fiscal transparency, accountability, and efficiency, building a more robust and resilient fiscal framework. Key initiatives in this endeavor include:

Integrated Financial Management System (IFMS): This system represents a significant step towards modernizing and streamlining public financial management, making it more transparent and efficient.

Treasury Single Account (TSA): The TSA will serve as a central reservoir, consolidating government cash balances, improving cash management, and enhancing control over budget execution.

Reassurance for Investors: A Steady Hand on the Tiller

The government's proactive and multifaceted approach to navigating these fiscal challenges, should instil confidence in investors. By taking concrete steps to control expenditure, diversify revenue sources, and strengthen fiscal management practices, the government is demonstrating its commitment to fiscal responsibility – creating a more stable, predictable, and attractive environment for investment.

While the fiscal landscape presents inherent challenges, the government's unwavering dedication to reform and its focus on long-term sustainability serve as a beacon for investors seeking to capitalize on Iraq's vast and largely untapped potential.

Favourable Investment Climate: Unearthing the Treasures of Opportunity

Iraq emerges as a land brimming with promise, offering a favorable climate for investment and a wealth of untapped opportunities for businesses with a thirst for adventure and an eye for potential.

Here's a glimpse of what makes Iraq a compelling destination for those seeking to stake their claim:

Competitive Tax Regime: Reaping the Rewards of a Favorable Fiscal Landscape

Competitive Edge: Iraq boasts a tax structure that stands out in the region, with competitive corporate and individual tax rates, making it a haven for businesses seeking to optimize their tax burden and maximize returns.

Potential for a Brighter Horizon: The report hints at the potential for further enhancements to the tax landscape, mentioning "payroll tax reform" and a "review of customs duties," signaling a commitment to creating an even more business-friendly environment. These reforms could encompass simplifying the tax code, reducing rates, and streamlining administration – music to the ears of investors.

Attracting Global Capital: A competitive tax regime acts as a powerful magnet, drawing foreign investment and fueling economic growth. By reducing the cost of doing business, Iraq is positioning itself as an attractive destination for global capital.

Attractive Investment Requirements: Smoothing the Path to Success

Streamlined Procedures: The government has rolled out the welcome mat for investors, implementing policies designed to streamline investment procedures and dismantle bureaucratic roadblocks, making it easier for businesses to set up shop and thrive.

Ease of Doing Business: Attractive capital and investment requirements, often sweetened with incentives tailored for foreign investors, make Iraq a fertile ground for businesses to take root. These incentives can include tax breaks, subsidies, and expedited licensing procedures – the fertilizer for rapid growth.

Investor Confidence: A transparent and predictable investment framework is the bedrock upon which investor confidence is built. By establishing clear rules of the game and adhering to international best practices, Iraq is fostering an environment that encourages long-term investment and sustainable growth.

Untapped Potential: A Frontier of Opportunity Awaits

First-Mover Advantage: As a nation rebuilding its economy and infrastructure, Iraq presents a frontier of opportunity, a landscape ripe for those with the vision and courage to seize the moment. Early investors have the potential to establish a dominant market presence, build brand recognition, and secure access to valuable resources and talent – reaping the rewards of being ahead of the curve.

Growth Potential: The ongoing reconstruction and development efforts are akin to igniting a powerful engine of economic growth. This momentum is expected to generate significant opportunities across a multitude of sectors in the coming years, creating a rising tide that will lift those who dare to ride it.

In addition to these compelling factors, Iraq's strategic location at the crossroads of trade, its young and growing population brimming with potential, and its abundant natural resources combine to create an irresistible allure for investors seeking to diversify their portfolios and tap into a market on the cusp of transformation. By embracing a strategic approach, leveraging the government's commitment to reform, and harnessing the power of local partnerships, investors can position themselves at the forefront of this dynamic and evolving market, reaping the rewards of their foresight and contributing to the dawn of a new era of prosperity for Iraq

Opportunities Amidst Transition: Riding the Crest of Change

Specific sectors ripe for growth and transformation, revealing a treasure map of lucrative opportunities for investors savvy enough to navigate Iraq's evolving landscape. Let's set our compasses and chart a course towards these promising horizons:

Digitalization: Powering Up Iraq's Digital Frontier

Iraq's digital landscape is experiencing a thrilling surge of activity, fueled by increasing internet penetration, a young and tech-savvy population eager to embrace the digital world, and the government's proactive push towards a digital-first economy.

This convergence of factors has created a fertile valley brimming with opportunities for businesses operating in the digital space.

Fintech Boom: The report highlights the government's commitment to ushering in a new era of digital payments and financial inclusion – music to the ears of fintech innovators. This burgeoning sector is ripe for companies offering game-changing solutions:

Mobile Payments: Providing convenient and accessible payment solutions, empowering a population with limited access to traditional banking services to participate fully in the digital economy.

Digital Banking: Revolutionizing the banking experience by offering online services, including account opening, money transfers, and bill payments, reaching a wider customer base and driving financial inclusion.

Online Lending: Breaking down barriers to credit by facilitating access for individuals and businesses through online platforms, leveraging alternative credit scoring models to unlock financial opportunities.

E-commerce and Digital Services: As internet penetration soars and the digital economy expands, a constellation of opportunities emerges for businesses providing:

E-commerce Platforms: Building vibrant online marketplaces to connect buyers and sellers, removing geographical barriers and fueling the growth of online retail.

Digital Marketing Services: Empowering businesses to navigate the digital landscape and reach their target audience through innovative online channels, including social media marketing, search engine optimization, and compelling content creation.

Online Entertainment: Capturing the hearts and minds of a digitally engaged population by providing captivating streaming services, engaging online gaming platforms, and other forms of digital entertainment, catering to the insatiable appetite for online content.

Data Centers and IT Infrastructure: The insatiable demand for digital services requires a robust and reliable IT infrastructure, creating a gold rush for businesses specializing in:

Data Centers: Building and operating state-of-the-art data centers, providing the secure and reliable data storage and processing power essential for a thriving digital economy.

Cloud Computing: Offering flexible and scalable cloud-based services, such as software-as-a-service (SaaS), platform-as-a-service (PaaS), and infrastructure-as-a-service (IaaS), enabling businesses to access computing resources on demand and scale their operations with agility.

Cybersecurity: Safeguarding businesses and individuals in the digital realm, providing essential services like robust network security, impenetrable data encryption, and proactive threat intelligence to counter the evolving landscape of cyber threats.

Renewable Energy: Harnessing the Power of a Sustainable Future

Iraq is embarking on an ambitious journey towards a cleaner, greener future, seeking to reduce its dependence on fossil fuels and transition to a more sustainable energy mix. This paradigm shift presents a wealth of opportunities for investors eager to capitalize on the renewable energy revolution.

Decarbonization Drive: The report underscores Iraq's unwavering commitment to decarbonization, a journey towards reducing its reliance on fossil fuels and embracing a cleaner energy future. This opens a treasure chest of opportunities for investors in renewable energy technologies:

Solar Energy: Harnessing the power of Iraq's abundant sunlight, a resource as vast as its deserts, to generate clean electricity through solar photovoltaic (PV) systems and concentrated solar power (CSP) plants.

Wind Energy: Utilizing Iraq's wind resources, capturing the energy of the desert winds to generate electricity through strategically placed wind turbines, particularly in areas where nature provides a constant and powerful breeze.

Hydropower: Exploring the untapped potential of hydropower generation from dams and rivers, a particularly promising avenue in the water-rich northern regions of Iraq.

Energy Efficiency Solutions: Improving energy efficiency emerges as a cornerstone of Iraq's decarbonization strategy, a golden opportunity for businesses offering cutting-edge energy-efficient technologies and services:

Smart Grids: Modernizing the electricity grid, transforming it into a dynamic and intelligent system capable of improving efficiency, enhancing reliability, and seamlessly integrating renewable energy sources.

Energy Audits: Acting as energy detectives, assessing energy consumption patterns in buildings and industries to identify areas for improvement, uncovering hidden savings and optimizing energy use.

Building Retrofits: Like breathing new life into aging structures, upgrading existing buildings with energy-efficient technologies can significantly reduce energy consumption and costs. This presents a wealth of opportunities for businesses specializing in advanced insulation, energy-saving lighting systems, and high-efficiency HVAC systems.

Green Finance and Investment: Sowing the Seeds of a Sustainable Future

The transition to a low-carbon economy requires more than just innovation; it demands a significant influx of capital. This creates fertile ground for:

Green Finance Institutions: These institutions play a crucial role in nurturing a greener future by providing the financial fuel for renewable energy projects and sustainable infrastructure development, driving the transition to a more sustainable model.

Impact Investors: These forward-thinking investors are drawn to ventures that generate both financial returns and a positive impact on the planet and its people. They find fertile ground in Iraq, investing in companies and projects committed to environmental sustainability and social responsibility.

By capitalizing on these emerging trends and aligning their investments with Iraq's long-term vision, businesses have the opportunity to not only generate attractive financial returns but also play a pivotal role in shaping a more sustainable and prosperous future for the nation. The digitalization and renewable energy sectors, in particular, shimmer with immense growth potential, beckoning investors to be part of Iraq's exciting journey of economic transformation.

Key Takeaways for Investors: A Compass for Navigating the Iraqi Market

Investing in Iraq is akin to embarking on an expedition into a land of both promise and challenge. Here are the essential landmarks to keep in mind:

1. **Due Diligence: Charting a Course Through the Fiscal Landscape**

Oil Price Volatility: Acknowledging the unpredictable nature of the oil market, and projecting a potential decline in oil prices over the medium term, a ripple effect that could impact government revenue and spending. Wise investors should meticulously assess the potential impact of oil price fluctuations on their projects, particularly those closely intertwined with government funding or oil revenue.

Fiscal Risks: Shy not away from the fiscal challenges ahead, highlighting a widening budget deficit and a rising tide of public debt. Investors would be wise to carefully analyze the government's fiscal policies and debt sustainability, assessing the potential impact on their investment horizons.

Project-Specific Analysis: Just as an explorer meticulously studies maps before venturing into uncharted territory, investors should conduct thorough due diligence on specific projects, carefully considering factors like regulatory approvals, land acquisition, environmental impact, and social considerations to chart a course towards success.

2.   Partnerships: Forging Alliances for Success

Navigating the Regulatory Labyrinth: Collaborating with local partners, those intimately familiar with the intricacies of the Iraqi regulatory landscape, can be akin to having a seasoned guide navigating a complex maze. Local partners provide invaluable expertise on legal requirements, licensing procedures, and compliance matters, smoothing the path for foreign investors.

Leveraging Local Knowledge: Local partners, like wise sages, possess in-depth knowledge of the market, cultural nuances, and business practices – invaluable assets for navigating this dynamic terrain. They can act as catalysts for market entry, identify potential customers and suppliers, and build bridges with key stakeholders.

Joint Ventures and Strategic Alliances: Forming joint ventures or strategic alliances with local companies is akin to forging a powerful expedition team, pooling resources and expertise. These collaborations provide access to established distribution networks, a wealth of local knowledge, and an immediate foothold in the market.

3. Long-Term Vision: Setting a Course for Sustainable Growth

Economic Diversification: Economic diversification is not merely a goal but a necessity for Iraq's long-term prosperity. Investors should prioritize projects that contribute to the growth of non-oil sectors, nurturing a more resilient and multifaceted economy.

Private Sector Growth: Recognizing the private sector as the engine of sustainable growth, the report highlights the need for structural reforms to unleash its full potential. Investors should prioritize projects that empower a vibrant and competitive private sector, creating jobs, fostering innovation, and driving economic expansion.

Sustainable Development: Investors have a unique opportunity to align their investments with Iraq's sustainable development goals, leaving a positive legacy. By prioritizing projects that champion clean energy, resource efficiency, and social inclusion, investors contribute to a brighter future for both Iraq and the planet.

By embracing these key takeaways, investors can confidently navigate the intricate tapestry of the Iraqi market, turning potential pitfalls into stepping stones, and transforming perceived risks into rewards. With a blend of strategic foresight, local expertise, and a commitment to sustainable growth, investors can unlock the treasure chest of Iraq's vast potential and contribute to its remarkable journey of transformation.

Chapter Conclusion: Iraq – Where Promise Meets Potential

This chapter has journeyed through the evolving tapestry of Iraq's business landscape. While acknowledging the looming shadows of fiscal challenges, including a widening deficit and the weight of rising public debt, the potential for growth and diversification that shimmers beneath the surface cannot be ignored.

The government's unwavering commitment to reconstruction and rehabilitation, particularly in the realm of infrastructure, unfurls a multi-billion-dollar tapestry of opportunity for international businesses. Meanwhile, the resolute push for diversification beyond the oil fields, fueled by transformative structural reforms and global initiatives like the BRI, opens doors to a vibrant array of sectors, beckoning businesses to sow the seeds of prosperity in agriculture, manufacturing, renewable energy, and services.

However, navigating this dynamic landscape demands more than just enthusiasm; it requires a compass calibrated for strategic decision-making. Investors must embark on a journey of thorough due diligence, carefully assessing the lay of the land, considering fiscal risks, and factoring in the unpredictable tides of oil price volatility. Partnering with local experts, those intimately familiar with the terrain, can prove invaluable, providing guidance through the labyrinth of regulatory requirements and unlocking the treasure trove of local knowledge. Most importantly, investors must adopt a long-term perspective, aligning their ambitions with Iraq's overarching development goals – a symphony of economic diversification, private sector empowerment, and sustainable growth.

Iraq stands at a pivotal crossroads, balancing the weight of its fiscal challenges with the exhilarating promise of a brighter future. For investors with the vision to recognize its potential, the resilience to navigate its complexities, and the commitment to embrace a long-term perspective, Iraq offers a unique and potentially lucrative opportunity to contribute to its economic renaissance and reap the rewards of its remarkable journey of transformation.

Bahaa G Arnouk

References

- IMF Country Report No. 24/280 on Saudi Arabia

- IMF Country Report No. 24/43 on Qatar

- IMF Country Report No. 24/31 on Oman

- IMF Country Report No. 23/223 on UAE

- IMF Country Report No. 23/331 on Kuwait

- IMF Country Report No. 24/128 on Iraq